St Ives Heritage

ERRATA

(1) The photographs on pages 13, 19, 23, 35, 47, 59, 61 and 99 are by
    S. H. Green, not F. H. Green as stated.
(2) Apologies to Peran Bray for misspelling his name.
(3) Chapter III starts on page 39, not 31 as stated on the Contents page.

Photograph opposite: Barnoon Hill, St Ives, 1904

Front cover: St Ives Harbour, photographed in 1903 by Herbert Hughes

(Both pictures courtesy RIC)

St Ives Heritage

Lena and Donald Bray

Recollections and Records of St Ives, Carbis Bay and Lelant

First published 1981 by Dyllansow Truran
Second edition, fully revised, first published 1992 by
LANDFALL PUBLICATIONS
Landfall, Penpol, Devoran, Truro, Cornwall
Telephone Truro (0872) 862581

A CIP catalogue record for this book is available from the British Library.

ISBN 1 873443 06 4

PUBLISHER'S NOTE

I first met Lena and Donald Bray as a result of writing a book of walks and local history, *A View from Trencrom*. Donald had kindly agreed to let me include an extract from a poem he had written about Angarrack. Later, when I gave him a copy of the book, he and Lena invited me to tea, and it was then that I discovered they had jointly written a book about "Greater St Ives". I had never seen a copy: it has been out of print for several years, and second-hand copies seem to be hard to come by - probably because it is the sort of book people want to keep. I borrowed one of the two Donald and Lena had, and read it with mixed emotions. On the one hand, it was very frustrating that I had not been aware of this treasure-trove when I was researching the background to walks through Lelant and Carbis Bay, and around Towednack, Halsetown and Trencrom Hill. If only I had known earlier, for example, about the dramatic changes during the 1870s that transformed the Carbis Valley from a wasteland of derelict mines, "dumps and all", to a place "with every appearance of having been the gem of the region from time immemorial".... On the other hand, what a delight to discover a book that blended historical records, traditional tales and personal memories so successfully! Such a book deserves to be readily available once again.

I should like to take this opportunity to thank Mr Leonard Truran, who originally published *St Ives Heritage*, for permitting me to produce this revised edition, and for his very helpful advice to a complete novice in the field of publishing other people's writing than my own. Thanks, too, to the Royal Cornwall Museum for permission to use several photographs and other illustrations from the RIC collection; and to Mrs Mary Baker, who has gone to great trouble in order to provide previously unpublished photographs of St Ives. These beautiful studies were made between 1920 and 1927 by her father, F. H. Green.

Bob Acton

Typesetting by Bob Acton

Printed by the Troutbeck Press
and bound by R. Booth Ltd., Antron Hill, Mabe, Penryn, Cornwall

CONTENTS

DEDICATION OF SECOND EDITION:

To our Grandsons
PERRAN and ROBERT BRAY
Cornish Australians
who love their Father's Homeland

FOREWORD

When they were aged ten and eight our two older Australian grandsons, Daniel and Thomas, visited us here in Cornwall. They were so keen to discover their roots, that we wrote "St Ives Heritage" for them and dedicated it to them, and to all who love this corner of the Far South West as we do.

It is the story of St Ives, Carbis Bay and Lelant up to World War Two, largely as seen through their grandmother's eyes, and as is known by hearsay and from the records and many fascinating books about the ancient Borough and its people.

Bob Acton, author and publisher of that fascinating series "Landfall Walks Books", liked "St Ives Heritage", long out of print, and handsomely undertook to reprint it, revised and updated to the 'nineties. Still, it remains much as it was when it went into many homes in the St Ives Bay area, and found its way to West Cornwall migrants the world over.

We would dedicate this second edition to our other grandsons, Perran and Robert, Australian born and aged ten and nine, who stayed with us last summer and also identify themselves with their father's native shores.

A bibliography is appended, and we gratefully acknowledge our indebtedness to those authors who have made so rich a study of St Ives. Little has been written about Carbis Bay and Lelant, and it has been a labour of love to repair the omission as best we can.

Our heartfelt thanks to Bob and his wife Viv for their interest, advice and judgement, and their unsparing devotion to launching our book once again among West Cornwall's expanding population.

LENA AND DONALD BRAY

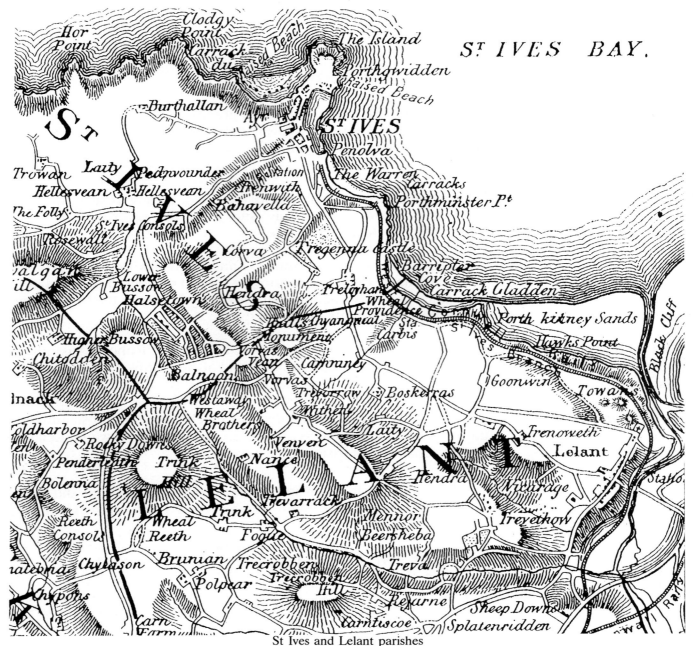

St Ives and Lelant parishes
as mapped soon after the opening of the St Ives Branch railway line (1877)

CHAPTER I

BACK'LONG

I have visited many beautiful, faraway places, and on each return I have stopped a little below St Anta Church at Carbis Bay to savour harbour, Island and the blue, blue sea of home. It is just there, as I round the bend on Porthrepta Road, that the impact of the view strikes me like a visual "lost chord" - a sensation of arresting delight seen as if never before. If the illusion of a first viewing fades as I gaze, and familiar features come one by one into focus, it is still the loveliest scene I ever set eyes on. This "lost chord" rediscovered at every homecoming is the experience of all I know who live here, and it brings our visitors back to us time and again.

The fisherman's view of the land as he comes in from the sea is less dramatic, rich rather in the highly individual story of this wide sweep of bay from Godrevy lighthouse to Pendinas Head. Hayle estuary lies in the middle with the sands and cliffs of Hayle and Gwithian away to the east, and nearer the river the rolling towans, or dunes, with their settlements of caravans and chalets, and homes and buildings of an industrial area. Inland are the busy towns of Camborne and Redruth and the headgear of South Crofty tin mine; an interesting if not particularly attractive scene, although Carn Brea with its castle at one end and towering monument at the other is both of these. But the view westward is as satisfying as you would expect - St Ives, Carbis Bay and Lelant with their valleys and trees and pretty houses, while a forest of rhododendrons, gorgeous in June blossoming, carpets the hill behind right up to the strange steeple on the summit.

St Ives, Carbis Bay and Lelant - Greater St Ives they called it when extending Borough boundaries in 1935. It is with these three places, once united in a single parish, then separated, and now one again, that this story deals. I was born in St Ives. It has developed a lot in my time, although until the last quarter of the 1800s several generations of my people had known little change there. My father used to say that until the building boom of the '80s, when St Ives began to spread across the steep sides of the Stennack valley and beyond, the sound of a hammer had hardly been heard in the town for sixty years.

When I was a year old we moved to Carbis Bay, where all my mother's relations lived. We seem to have been regarded by the townsfolk as country cousins; certainly we were more free of the taboos which persisted in such a close-knit, interrelated community as St Ives once was, and to some extent still is. The story of St Ives has been told before, but more has to be made of Carbis Bay, now its nearest suburb, and of Lelant. St Ives once belonged to the parish of Lelant and was in all ways the junior partner. The little fishing port only came into its own when the port of Lelant, in the Hayle estuary, silted up. It was to grow into one of the two principal harbours (Padstow was the other one) along the magnificent but treacherous north coast of the South West peninsula between Bideford and Lands End, while for ten years in the last century it achieved the distinction of a port of registry.

St Uny Lelant, built in the 12th century, is the mother church of St Ives, which apart from an oratory and a tiny chapel or two had no church of its own until three hundred years later. Bitter dissension arose from St Ives worshippers, when church-going was compulsory, having to trudge three miles to Lelant and back in all weathers each Sunday and holy day, besides repeating the journey for baptisms and weddings and funerals. It was particularly hard on the elderly, and indeed on anybody suffering from the various crippling diseases of those hard times. Women also had to take the long trail to be churched. For burial in Lelant churchyard the mourners had to carry the corpse along the whole of the "church way", a footpath which in places skirted the cliff edge. It was a perilous walk in a howling gale; sometimes they could not get to church at all. Wheeled vehicles were unknown in West Cornwall then, while until 1703 no-one bothered about road-making either. The church way was punctuated by granite blocks at stiles and such convenient spots, on which to lay the body and give the exhausted bearers a rest.

These labours were to be questioned by the growing and increasingly articulate population of St Ives, which was already matching Lelant in importance. In 1409 the townsfolk petitioned the Pope, through the good offices of Lord Champernown - a local landowner - to license a church of their own. They complained that because the church way was mountainous and rocky, and liable in winter to sudden inundations, they often could not attend church, baptise their children, church their women or bury their dead. What Pope could resist such pleas, particularly since they would build at their own expense and with their own labour? The licence was granted, the Archbishop of Canterbury and the Bishop of Exeter followed with theirs, and work commenced. Only the clergy at Lelant disapproved. Considering the fees they would lose, it was to be expected.

Everybody contributed either in labour or in money. There was wealth in the town to support the venture, as you have only to look at the noble building to see. A lucrative trade had been established with Ireland and Brittany. St Ia's arose on the site of the saint's ancient oratory, its granite being quarried at Zennor and transported by sea. It was thus that the harbour piers were built well into modern times, too, despite granite quarries in the neighbourhood. Shipment was easier and cheaper than hauling the blocks overland. The church was completed, all but the tower and the Trenwith aisle, in sixteen and a half years, a tribute to selfless toil and skill and open-handed devotion. When Bishop Lacy consecrated the new church on St Ia's feast day, 3rd February, in 1434, he named two other patrons besides the virgin saint - St Peter and his brother St Andrew.

Nobody needs telling about Peter and Andrew; but who apart from us locals knows anything about Ia? When I tell you that she was wafted across the Celtic Sea on a leaf you will either think me simple or accuse me of thinking that you are! Yet in a way that is just how she did arrive. For how otherwise would the handful of natives who lived above Porthminster Beach in the fifth century AD describe an Irish coracle, the likes of which they had never seen before, floating to shore for all the world like an outsized withered leaf with its sides curled up?

To Charles Henderson, who in his thirty-three years extracted so much living history from landscape and stones and yellowing parchment, Ia the Virgin was an entirely real person, whatever the Heavenly Appointments Board of the Vatican may say of saints such as she. An Irish chieftain's daughter, she may have been the sister of Uny and was certainly the friend of Piala, two of the many martyrs designate in the 700-strong expedition which Piala's brother Prince Fingar (or Gwinear) was leading to Armorica, which became Brittany after the Cornish migrations. These converts of the Welshman St Patrick were animated by both missionary zeal and an intention to colonise, and none was more zealous than Ia, but Fingar refused to take her. So Ia followed on her own. That is the sort of determined, dedicated soul she was.

She drifts into Hayle bay (there is no St Ives until it takes her name) while the expedition is still at sea. Contrary winds carry Fingar's flotilla not to Armorica but into the bay too, and he comes ashore to find Ia comfortably settled, resentful of her exclusion from the party, and by no means disposed to share her little group of proselytes with anybody else. So the seven hundred swarm across the Hayle river to Connor Downs, to be treated not without cause as a foray by the local heathen monarch, Teudar, and scattered. Fingar himself struggles to Gwinear with a frightful neck wound (tradition insists, "with his head tucked underneath his arm"!), Uny settles at Uny Lelant, Piala (romanised as Felicitas) is the St Phillack whose parish includes Hayle, and so it is with all the parishes within half an hour's drive of St Ives, traffic permitting. Some of these saints are sanctified in more habitations than one in the West Cornwall wilderness. To Ia, for instance, a cross stands in Camborne churchyard, while traces of her spiritual influence endure further afield, at Finisterre across the Channel.

Ia is real, all right, and a great deal was known about her at one time. The acts of the virgin saint used to be read from the pulpit of the new church on her Feast

Day. But alas! at the Reformation the Protestant vicar got rid of the manuscript along with her martyred bones. Nevertheless, we believe her to have brought the good people of St Ives to the pitch of religious certainty that they have defended ever since, and to have suffered martyrdom along with her hallowed compatriots at the hands of Teudar, who gets a rough deal from the monkish chroniclers in consequence. Her oratory, where the church stands, was built either in her lifetime or soon after. Her bones were venerated there for centuries and were transferred to the parish church, whence in the course of history they were no longer called upon to work miracles.

The town was kinder to Ia's memory than was the reforming vicar. At first known as Pendinas, the fort on the headland, it came to be called Ia's port, Porthia. Eventually it took the name of the parish, proceeding from Sancta Ye through Saynt Iyes and St Ithes until the "v" crept in and we get St Ives.

St Ives parish church is so close to the sea that from time to time, as I recall happening at evening service when I was a girl, a wave would hurtle against the churchyard wall, cascade over the high roof, and ooze down the main aisle. The St Ives historian, John Hicks, experienced a storm in 1697 which destroyed much of the roof together with the east window above the altar, but the church was not always so vulnerable. When Mr Hicks was fifteen, an old man remembered a field between churchyard and sea where sheep grazed. An old woman recalled "a great hurricane of the sea which happened at the beginning of the reign of King James I, when a considerable portion of St Ives was overwhelmed with sea and sand." This must have been the occasion when the sea "overwhelmed" the field and brought the tide up to the churchyard.

Mr Hicks, here quoted, was mayor of St Ives seven times in the twenty-seven years from 1688 to 1715, and he drew on the Borough archives for a detailed and reliable history which he completed in manuscript in 1722. The manuscript was used by the historian C. S. Gilbert a century later, since when it has vanished as utterly as the medieval St Ia manuscript. Surely, though, we may hope that the Hicks MS lies in some drawer, forgotten or indeed unrecognised, until better fortune restores its treasures to general use. But back

to the church and the sea at the door!

The construction of the "Lambeth Walk", the little promenade running from Westcott's Quay to the harbour, has since the 1930s preserved the church from such a pounding as has been described. Westcott's Quay, by the way, must be named after the Arthur Westcott who was for years a member of the Portreeve's Council and later of the Borough Council, and became a Warden of the Quay in 1636. As for the Lambeth Walk, my father in his aldermanic days used jocularly to refer to the new promenade as such when Lupino Lane's "Me and my Gal" penetrated to the far South West. It is amusing that the name is still used in place of the official Pednolva Walk!

The century of the building of the parish church brought St Ives into the main stream of history. Hitherto the story of the little port is obscure, lost in antiquity. There are signs that the natives may have defended themselves on the Island, as they did at Porthcurno and Gurnard's Head, against immigrants who came, not with cars and return tickets, but with metal swords and the intent to stay. Was St Ives there when the prehistoric villages flourished in the hinterland, at Chysauster, Goldherring and the like? Or did it come into being when the hill people at last found it relatively safe to descend to the coast?

Before the 15th century the inhabitants of St Ives had to trail to Lelant not only for their spiritual needs: the market was held there too. Just as the Lord Champernown had played a major part in getting St Ives its own church, his inheritor, Sir Robert Willoughby, did the like for its market. Sir Robert, afterwards Lord Broke, had been granted the manor of St Ives through marriage with the Champernown heiress. In 1488 he obtained a charter from Henry VII for a weekly market to be held in the town on Saturdays, together with two annual fairs. One of these survives, though barely: "fer-a-mogh", the pig fair, on November 30th, St Andrew's Day. Fer-a-mogh became Fairy Mo, and is now Fair Mo. When I was a girl, the pigs had gone and it was all fun and fairings - sugar almonds, macaroons and gingerbread. There were stalls lit with naphtha flares which leapt and writhed in the wind, and among the flickering shadows of the market place merrymaking was none the less hearty for being simple. Blackout and wartime put an end to all that, as they did to other of our Cornish customs and traditions, and nothing of Fair Mo is left but a bazaar in the church hall.

The Market House was built by Lord Broke in 1490, together with fortifications on the Island. It lasted for almost 350 years. In 1832 it was pulled down to make way for the building the traffic manoeuvres round today, with no greater ease than the Victorian traffic did. Until the present Guildhall took over in 1939 the upper storey of the Market House was the Borough's court room.

One August day in 1497 what a to-do there was in the little seaport! Joseph Polsue in Lake's Parochial History of Cornwall describes four warships sailing into the bay from Ireland, to disgorge no less a magnifico than the Pretender to the throne and his lady, with an escort of a hundred and fifty knights and men-at-arms. It was Richard of York and his duchess, the beautiful Katherine Gordon. Richard, it seemed, had escaped from the Tower of London, and after some years of preparation had landed to claim his throne from the Lancastrian usurper. The Pretender's followers proclaimed him King Richard IV in the market place, though I dare say that while not daring to show less than the utmost enthusiasm for the Pretender, the leading citizens were cagey as to what they committed themselves to. Leaving his lovely lady in the care of the monks at St Michael's Mount, the would-be monarch marched via Bodmin to Exeter, gathering adherents to his cause. A Cornish rebellion against excessive taxation - you can go so far against us Cornish and then no further - had just failed, though with such slight losses, except that the wretched leaders were hanged, drawn and quartered, that the Cousin Jacks were minded to try again. However, suffering a reverse at Exeter the Pretender ran away, leaving the Cornish to foot the bill. He proved to be Perkin Warbeck, a Burgundian commoner, and no more the Yorkist heir than the earlier impostor Lambert Simnel, so he really did find himself in the Tower. After an escape bid he was hanged. It is fair to add that more recent historians than Joseph Polsue maintain that Warbeck landed, not at St Ives but at Whitesand Bay near Lands End.

Perhaps he did, in which event there would still have been almost as big a stir in the Borough, while no doubt some of our young hotheads followed him to defeat.

Another insurrection had its echoes in St Ives fifty years later - the Prayer Book Rebellion. You might think that the Cornish were prone to tell their London masters where they got off, and probably you are right. The immortal words of "Trelawny" - the Cornish national anthem if ever there was one! - "Here's twenty thousand Cornishmen shall know the reason why", though applying to another incursion across the Tamar which, however, did not come off, pretty well sums it up.

The 1549 rebellion was sparked off by the over-hasty measures taken by Lord Protector Seymour, uncle of the boy King Edward VI, to replace the Catholic by the new Protestant beliefs and form of worship throughout the land. The Cornish were affronted at the changes in the devotions which formed such a part of their way of life. The new service was "but lyke a Christmas game." They would have it in Latin as before: "We, the Cornyshe men, whereof certen of us understa'de no Englysh, utterly refuse thys newe English." They would have images in every church and prayers for the dead. A King's Commissioner, suspected of having designs on the church plate, was murdered at Helston, and other acts of violence were committed; followed by hangings, drawings and quarterings when the perpetrators were rounded up.

At the Whitsunday service that fateful year, when the law required that the English prayer book be used throughout the kingdom for the first time, the South West rose in rebellion. For a while the law of the land was unenforceable in Cornwall, and when through July and August Cornish and South Devon rebels besieged Exeter, it seemed that the Catholic cause might prevail. After fierce fighting and desperate losses the besiegers were routed by government forces, and then the horrid tale of retribution began again on a far wider scale, though it was not the Protector's policy to wreak vengeance on the common folk: his quarry was those who had led them. So Provost Marshal, the singularly odious Anthony Kingston, was let loose on Cornwall to hang numerous priests and citizens who

St Ives in the 1920s   (Photograph by F. H. Green)

had been in any way concerned with the insurrection.

John Payne, Portreeve of St Ives, was one of these. When Kingston visited the town he was entertained by the portreeve at the George and Dragon, a hostelry which stood in the market place where the butcher's and chemist's shops are today, and was patronised by the best people in the neighbourhood. The amiable discourse between the two dignitaries was punctuated by hammering as, at the Provost Marshal's request, a scaffold was erected outside. A hearty dinner having been enjoyed by both, Mr Payne, by now convinced that the not very considerable part he had played in the affair had been overlooked, conducted his guest to the gallows.

"Are they strong enough?" Sir Anthony enquires.

"Doubtless they are," Mr Payne assures him, clasping his hands across his ample stomach.

"Then get up speedily," says the Provost, "for they are prepared for you."

"I hope," gasps the Portreeve in that awful moment of truth, "you mean not as you speak."

"In faith," he is told, "there is no remedy, for you have been a busy rebel."

And so concludes another episode in the history of the market place. It has been commemorated in recent years by a plaque on the wall of the Catholic church at the top of Tregenna Hill.

This cat and mouse approach to his victim seems to have been a ploy of the Provost Marshal. He hanged the Mayor of Bodmin after a similar reception; yet His Worship was not even the rebel mayor, a prime mover of the rebellion! He had succeeded him at mayor choosing. Justice reasserted itself, it is gratifying to know, in the next reign, Mary's. Kingston, charged with planning to rob the exchequer, poisoned himself to avoid the even harsher penalty of the law.

The market place at St Ives was pretty grim in days gone by, as most market places were. The town gaol, a noisome den, was under the Market House (a small fort near the present museum served as a prison too); the stocks stood outside the church; and there was a cage for imprisoning an offender in the unremitting view of the populace. There was a whipping post, where "the maid that would drown herself," poor creature, was publicly thrashed. The fellow who administered it got sixpence for the job. A man and a woman were whipped at a shilling a time, another man at sixpence, a couple of women together at half a crown. Was there a tariff for the number of lashes, I wonder? Did better class miscreants like "William Nance's wife" get first class treatment at first class prices? The Borough archives list many more occasions of this barbarous punishment that was last administered not so very long ago. Of course, there was the "cuckingstool", or ducking stool, for the correction of scolds. This though was erected on the wharf. Up with the beam shoreside and down the seesaw goes, splash and under! Great fun for all except the wife who had spoken a mouthful too much!

The market place again witnessed a spectacle of painful entertainment when my father was a boy. A quack came to town advertising the first painless extractions ever, and set up his stall there. A team of local lads equipped with tin cans was assembled and briefed. Then came the public pronouncement, "Teeth out - you won't feel a thing!" The sufferers lined up, the pincers were flourished, and to cheers and the beating of cans which drowned all sounds else the offending molar was held up like the heart of an Inca sacrifice for the approval of the crowd. Next please! And there probably was a "next" and more too. The first victim got his extraction free, on the understanding that he would declare it painless; while the rest of the patients, whose yells no-one had heard, were not going to confess themselves less manly than their predecessors in the seat of torment. Besides, it was common enough in the Far West when Queen Victoria reigned to get a "horse doctor", or even a blacksmith, to take your tooth out. So probably the expert quack gave a good and necessary service.

The "busy rebel" John Payne had been a portreeve. His successor ninety years afterwards became a mayor, when the dignity of incorporation was bestowed upon the town and St Ives became a borough. It had already,

whenever the spirit moved, and by immigrant shopkeepers anxious to offer the visitors a seven-day service.

But back to another gift, with seal and cup the third, which was made to the new Borough to mark its inauguration. This was the pair of silver maces inscribed with the name of the donor, Richard Hext. They still precede His Worship on ceremonial occasions. As for the seal, it went missing during the Commonwealth and was replaced in 1690. That is the one we have now.

In its earliest days the Borough of St Ives had problems to cope with on a scale never to be equalled again. From the outbreak of Civil War in 1642 to '44 blank pages are all there are to show of the Borough records. There were matters of greater moment to think about. St Ives with its Puritan leadership was out of step with almost every other town in the West, the townsfolk being more disposed to follow Mayor Stevens, the Ceely brothers, the Sises, who were a rich and influential merchant family extinct, I am told, these past three hundred years, Captain Francis Arundell and other Parliamentarians. These republican leanings were the more clearly defined when the inhabitants struggled to raise the levy for the King's Cornish regiments. This levy amounted to nearly two hundredweight of food a day in meat, dairy produce and bread, the first two items luxury and the last precious to most of the town's 1500 population, who had little to spare at the best of times.

1645 was as critical a year for St Ives in the South West as it was for King Charles in the country. The Borough declared for Parliament, whereupon the King's General of the West, Sir Richard Grenville (he was the grandson of the *Revenge* hero) hurried sou'west and scattered St Ives Roundheads on Longstone Downs, between Carbis Bay and Lelant. Then he took up residence with the Mayor, Edward Hammond, who must have nurtured disquieting recollections of what transpired after John Payne's entertainment of a King's officer a hundred years before. However, Mayor Hammond got away with what was for those days the enormous fine of £400, though it was not until he had cooled his heels in Launceston gaol for three

months that he would pay up. Captain Arundell, who had led the vanquished Roundheads, escaped by sea to Bridgwater, where he joined the Parliamentary General Fairfax. In St Ives a Zennor constable named Phillips was hanged, while a couple of the townspeople were removed, one to Helston and the other to Truro, and hanged there, doubtless to avoid the riot which would have attended their execution on home ground.

That the town's preference for Parliament had been quelled rather than quenched became apparent as soon as Grenville and his troops returned to the mainstream of the war. The Roundheads took over the town again. The dashing cavalry commander Colonel Goring was despatched to teach St Ives an even severer lesson. However, it was the Colonel who learnt it. He was held at bay at the town's approaches by barricades of pilchard barrels filled with sand, manned by citizens desperate in the knowledge of the retribution which would follow failure. It was the Cavaliers who retreated.

The Ceely family came to the fore during the Civil War. William Ceely was a parliamentary commissioner for Cornwall. His brother Peter was a great uprooter of everything the Puritans held to savour of idolatry. He destroyed the medieval chapel over Madron Holy Well, and got rid of the organ and railings in St Ives church, together with the stained glass and the beautiful medieval rood-screen. He was a military man as well as an iconoclast, holding Cromwell's commission as major and later as Vice Admiral of the local seaways.

Great distress fell upon the town in 1647. Two blunt extracts from the resumed accounts read: "Received of Mr George Hicks upon Major Ceelye Tickatts for corne," and "payd to Major Ceelye towards the corne for Mr Opie £135." There was famine in St Ives, which arose from the town's being strictly quarantined for the greater part of the year. Plague had broken out in April. By October a third of the population were dead and half the survivors had contrived to flee the town. The remainder were severely isolated and arrangements for their sustenance were at best chancy. Provisions which came into St Ives from the countryside were now left beside streams at Polmantor beyond the Stennack and at Carbis Bay. Prices were attached; and when the vendors were well clear the food was collected and payment left in the stream with the water washing over it. The markets were closed, and there was no other source of supply. When the inhabitants were weakening from starvation a Plymouth ship belonging to a Mr Opie came into harbour, unaware of the closure of the port. What a welcome it received! The Mayor, Mr Thomas Sprigge, purchased its cargo of wheat and wine for £196 and distributed the wheat free. The wine was sold by the Corporation at twelve pence a quart. Had it not been for the solitary caller at a time when callers were otherwise non-existent, it is likely that more people would have perished of famine than of plague. The standard cure appears to have been a concoction of two penn'orth of brandy, a penn'orth of treacle, and water. It was said to be highly effective, at least with ague. Worth trying even now, perhaps, though I am not sure about the treacle!

An incident in the history of St Ives illustrated a fear which hung over every seaport in the realm during the long struggle with Napoleon. Miss Sarah Edwards was an old lady, a friend of one of my aunts, who died in 1959. She was a member of a Down'long family who kept a half-sovereign as an heirloom, and she told its story to the late Mr W. J. Jacobs, founder in 1899 and editor till retiring in 1955 of the Western Echo, who recorded it in his private journal. The press gang was making one of its frequent raids on St Ives. Usually prior warning enabled the young men to go to ground in their various hiding places, one of these being the "man-o'-war pit" on Trink Hill. However on this occasion the warning system had failed, and a likely young sailor the gang had had word of fled to his mother's house near the harbour. His mother barred the door and sent him upstairs. Hot on his trail the naval men demanded admittance, whereupon his mother armed herself with a rolling pin and swore to brain the first man to cross her doorstep. Nevertheless, the door was battered in and the officer commanding the press gang stepped over the threshold. Down came the rolling pin, and the officer staggered back with a broken arm. However his men rushed the house and seized the young man, not to be heard of again until hostilities ceased. With the coming of peace a naval flotilla put into Falmouth, whereupon the mother walked all the way there to seek news of her boy. His ship, she learned, was one of those at anchor in the harbour. Ignoring warnings as to her personal safety, she went on board and found her son. It was a joyful reunion, which ended in despair when the officer sent for her, but to her astonishment he made her welcome, said he admired her pluck and gave her a half-sovereign. That was the heirloom.

THE CHURCH OF ST IA

Beside an alien harbour stands
The church. Not its the holiday-
Homes and shops, unsullied sands
Where all the catch a fisherman lands
Is trippers round the Bay.

Time was, it topped a thousand thin
Mastheads of lugger, schooner, barque;
The Bay was fish, the land was tin
Till with the trains the world flocked in
And wharf was pleasure park.

Time was, the church of Ia saw
Knights parade to proclaim a king;
A portreeve hanged; and on the shore
Pirates, Turks and Frenchmen pour
Burning and plundering.

It hid the trade of midnight beach
Under its walls from Custom's search;
Watched wild seas its glebeland breach;
In Market Place heard Wesley preach.
(They said he'd wreck the church!)

Hark, the knock of axe and maul
On yellowed scroll through ages brought!
Yo-ho-heave! The townsmen haul
Granite blocks up the mounting, tall
Tower above the port.

Give, the word went, what you can;
Burgher, a tithe of all you own!
Carve the oak, craftsman! Build and plan
Master, 'prentice and journeyman!
Boatman, ferry the stone!

They built this church as now you see
By skill and back-break, fish and tin;
Up-country accents rouse the quay -
And gulls; the porch is wide for me
And it is quiet within.

Fishing boats at St Ives, 1920s (Photograph by F. H. Green)

Outside the Sloop Inn, St Ives, 1904
(Photograph by J. C. Burrow, courtesy RIC)

CHAPTER II

MOSTLY DOWN'LONG

My outstanding childhood recollection of St Ives harbour is the all-pervading smell of fish. The boats came in with the night's catch, brimming to the gunnels when luck was with them. You would stand at the pierhead and watch the sunlight or the lamplight, as might be, glinting on the silvery horde as the boats heaved home on the swell. Then there was the unloading into skiffs and dinghies, or at ebb tide into carts. The harbour beach was littered with discarded scraps of ray, and of dogfish which played havoc with the nets and were spiked on hooks and skinned, thereupon achieving status as rock salmon, an up-country delicacy shunned at home.

The fish market was held on the wharf, at the top of the lifeboat slip after the new road was made. In the season you would see the animated and surprisingly cheerful scene, when you consider what a raw-armed job it was, of local girls and fishwives, and also of lassies imported all the way from Scotland, preparing herring for the smoke-house or packing the pilchards in barrels - a layer of fish and a handful of coarse salt. These were pressed in the fish cellars for export, mainly to Italy and the Mediterranean. The resultant oil was a secondary export. Among other purposes it was used - can you believe it? - for the manufacture of cosmetics. But much of it finished up in little saucers called "chills", feeding a wick and glimmering smokily in the kitchen of the country people of Penwith. Marinaded pilchards, a St Ives and for that matter a Cornish speciality, were exported too. I quote my cousin Mary's recipe:
"Pilchards are an excellent savoury especially hot for breakfast. After cleaning, top and tail the fish and place in a cloam bowl, all head-ends one way and tail-ends in alternate layers. Sprinkle each layer with salt, powdered mixed spice and bay leaves. Slowly add common vinegar, never the best or malted vinegar. This preparation must not boil; place in a very slow oven or cool oven overnight and serve warm for breakfast. Everything is edible, even the bones."

Until about the end of World War One St Ives women took their bowls of fish to one of the local bake-houses for overnight baking.

Every cottage had its cellar for barking nets and sails and stowing crab pots and the like. There were cellars for storing fish and smoke-houses for kippering them. Tommy Taylor Uren is still remembered in his chimney with the kippers strung up as high in the smoke as you could see. It was sawdust smoke, different sorts of sawdust for the various stages in the process, the harbour boat-yards supplying it in abundance. And what kippers they were! None of your impregnated herring painted up like a chorus girl! On each cottage wall "tow-rag" hung on a nail to bleach. Tow-rag was white dried fish, a favourite among St Ives folk who in common with most seafaring people had little taste for fresh fish, no doubt because they saw, handled and smelt so much of it, and lived on it, perforce, when in their boats at sea. But salt pilchards were popular Down'long because it was supposed they cured rheumatism.

Everywhere in the open were seagulls, wheeling and screaming and swooping as the offal was flung on to the sands; while in the narrow streets and alleyways cats munched the fruits of their foraging. The old riddle-me-ree when "As I was going to St Ives .... each wife had seven cats" is not without substance. Though I would not say as much for the line preceding! Gulls and cats used to be the town's scavengers. They kept the wharf clean enough, though the smell remained. The gulls are still as numerous - the visitors see to that. Adapting themselves to a human diet rather than fish, fishing being in decline, they greet the dawn from our roof-tops rather than from their nooks and niches in the cliffs, and intimidate visitors, while the Council plans counter-measures. But thanks to cars and a shifting population there are fewer cats.

Life at St Ives has always revolved around the harbour.

It does today, even though gaily painted pleasure boats have largely replaced the sombre but indelibly romantic fishing boats with trips round the bay or along the coast to Seal Island: though fish cellars and boat-builders' workshops, thanks to the touch of your modern architect, have been magicked into restaurants, Woolworth's and gift shops: though fishermen's cottages have been gutted to make way for expensive flats and residences, only the traditional exteriors remaining as they were, while some of their owners, rather on the lines of Marie Antoinette's shepherdesses at Trianon, don peaked caps and expect to pass off as sons of the sea. The harbour foreshore, with coal dust - coal being a regular cargo for the mines and domestic use - oil, tarry patches and fragments too repulsive even for the gulls to swallow, used to be no place for lying out in the sun. But now it is one of the resort's most popular beaches. Fishing, which earned our fishermen over £50,000 in the twenties, had declined to £5,000's worth within ten years. It was like the collapse of mining, except that while the miners had travelled the world in search of work the fishing community stayed at home and opened its homes, and at last sold them, to visitors.

Despite the many changes the years have wrought, the harbour has preserved, even enhanced, its charm: though perhaps this is rather more continental now than "old world". Until 1922 the wharf road was so narrow as to bring the ships right up to the front door, while the front door was but a stride to the water's edge - unrailed, too, railings not then having replaced common sense in the matter of brinkmanship. Often the tide lapped the doorsteps and splashed up into the alleyways. Then the road was widened and redesigned and a fine sea wall built.

With tourism becoming the main industry of the Borough, Wharf Road is hardly more than a promenade; a delightful one, but the harbour has lost its identity as a fishing haven. But there are still the fishermen's lodges to bespeak a vanishing generation while the lifeboat is as busy as ever; busier if you count the constant demand on the rubber inshore rescue boat which is a sign of the times. The old granite cottages look much as they have always done, except that the paintwork is brighter today and more varied, despite the District Council regulations to enforce a dull uniformity, than the drab browns and greens of my childhood - and the liberal coating of tar. There is still a labyrinth of roads a single fish-cart wide around the harbour. They go in all directions and bear the same old names - The Digey, Bethesda Place, Salubrious Place, Fish Street and so forth. The houses are so close together that before the fishing families dispersed "Up'long" the Cornish tendency to litigation was exercised to the full. There were constant arguments about "ancient lights" and ancient rights, and solicitors' letters circulated as freely as OHMS missives today.

Almost everyone and everything round the harbour had to do with the sea. When the fishing fleet was in, the harbour was a forest of masts, crammed with craft for the most part lugger-rigged, until after World War One a government scheme for the hire-purchase of engines obviated reliance on the wind but limited the choice of fishing grounds to the capacity of fuel tanks and the cost of petrol. Whenever the rocket summoning the lifeboat thudded above the roof-tops and dropped in dissolving brilliance, even women heaved waist-deep in angry seas as they helped drag the heavy carriage into the waves for launching. Everything from launch to rescue was done by muscle power when I was very young; the muscle power of the indomitable people of St Ives, attuned to seafaring since birth, and brought up in that love-hate relationship all coastwise folk feel for the sea most of them directly or indirectly live and too often die by.

Boys could "scully" with a single oar around the harbour moorings before they could tie their boot laces. In the absence of more conventional craft they would paddle about in their mothers' wash trays, kneeling and using their hands for propulsion. These wash trays were wooden rectangular tubs three feet long or so, the four sides sloping outwards. There was always a wash tray race in the harbour during the annual regatta. I recall a hip-bath entry sinking, spiralling to the bottom a couple of fathoms deep, followed down by the two nippers who manned it. They got it up! The local boys were taught to swim by drop them overboard, and come to the rescue only if the most desperate "dog's paddle" failed to keep head above water. It was a traumatic ordeal, a preparation for the stern life of a fishing port years ago.

Fish carts at St Ives, 1920s (Photograph by F. H. Green)

No-one is more proud of his home town than a St Ives man, nor with better reason. There is nothing in which he takes greater pride than the St Ives lifeboat. His town has been a lifeboat station since 1840, with an unsurpassed record for service and sacrifice. His proudest, and saddest, hour was early one Monday morning, 23rd January in that year of ill fate 1939. A force 10 nor'westerly storm was gusting up to almost 100 mph when, at 2.30 am, St Just coastguards reported a large steamship being overwhelmed by those tremendous breakers which a winter gale will roll in from the Atlantic wastes. Sennen lifeboat, the nearest, could not be launched because of low tide and great seas crashing at the foot of the slipway.

Coxwain Cocking and the lifeboat secretary met in the lifeboat house. I quote Secretary Guppy's evidence.
He said, "What's the news?"
I said, "Well, Tommy, the Sennen boat can't get out."
He said, "We're off!" and he immediately ran for the maroons. I would like to say here and now that there was no hesitation whatever on anybody's part about taking the boat out.
By 3 am ninety volunteers had dragged the lifeboat across the harbour sands and launched her. They had been waist deep in the chilling water, turbulent even in the lee of the Island, so that several were injured by being knocked under the cumbersome carriage or against the boat.

Rounding St Ives head, the lifeboat met a strong flood tide and the full rage of the sea. Off Clodgy it capsized, flinging five men into the sea. One, William Freeman, had retained his grip on the lifelines and was hauled aboard. A voice was heard shouting. It was Signalman John Thomas, the cries growing fainter as the boat drifted to leeward. The four survivors started up the engine, but a trailing rope fouled the propeller. Back off the Island they dropped anchor and burned distress flares. Then the new Manilla cable parted and they overturned again. Three men were now left on board. Entirely at the mercy of the mountainous seas the lifeboat drifted across the bay, and approaching the inner sound off Godrevy Point, capsized a third time. Only William Freeman remained. The waves smashed the boat down on the rocks, he stepped out, and his sharpened senses enabling him to see as clearly as if it were day,

scrambled out and up the cliff to raise the alarm. Mr Freeman was not a regular member of the crew; he had persuaded an older man who had 'flu, a family man, to give him his place in the boat.

Of the seven lifeboatmen who lost their lives, five had been survivors of the *Alba* disaster, when the St Ives lifeboat was wrecked a year before, almost to the day. They had gone to London to receive medals for gallantry from the RNLI President, the Duke of Kent. It was with a catch in his voice that my father, who accompanied the party, would recall finding a box for "Jan Spargo" Thomas, when chosen for interview at Broadcasting House, to stand on to reach the microphone. Jan Spargo, shortest member of the crew, had been scrum half and later full back for the "Chiefs". "Marlow", otherwise Matthew, and Willie Barber were former star members of the town's famous rugby XV too. The 1939 tragedy was the third occasion on which Coxwain Thomas Cocking had been flung into the raging sea when the lifeboat collapsed. Now he, his son and his son-in-law were drowned, as were both the Barber brothers. All the lost lifeboatmen were married, four of them each with two young children. The body of the indomitable coxwain (at sixty-four we would have considered him practically a pensioner today) was washed ashore far up the coast at Portreath. It was a sad yet heroic end to his forty-four years as a lifeboatman. As coxwain his annual salary had been - £16!

As for the vessel in distress, unknown and unheard, it was assumed she had hauled safely out to sea. Days later a wreck was spotted from the cliffs near Pendeen. It had been driven broadside on to the offshore rocks and everything abaft the bridge had been flattened as if by the heel of a giant. It was SS *Wilston,* with a crew of 30 of whom there was no trace; all 3,000 tons of her lifted by a giant roller that dashed her down to the rocks, breaking her back and giving no time to signal or lower her boats. This was surely the steamer the St Just coastguards had reported, the ship for which Thomas Cocking, Matthew Barber, Richard Stevens, John Cocking, John Thomas, William Barber and Edgar Basset sacrificed their lives, and for which William Freeman, the sole survivor, ended his days tormented by memories.

The St Ives Lifeboat "Covent Garden" (1870-78) ready for launching.
(Photographer unknown - possibly Edward Ashton. Courtesy RIC.)

Decoration at RNLI Headquarters of the *Alba* Lifeboatmen, May 1938
Left to right: Coxwain Thomas Cocking, William Peters, Matthew Barber, John Cocking, John Thomas,
Thomas Cocking Jnr., Henry Peters, William Barber, Philip Paynter.
Five were lost in the lifeboat disaster a year later.

The launching of SV *Baratanach* at St Ives Harbour
(Photograph by Edward Ashton, courtesy RIC)

Besides fishing vessels quite large ships moored in the harbour or tied up at the pier. They still do. Prior to 1770 only one pier existed. It extended from the Ship Aground Inn at Carn Glaze, the site of the present Fishermen's "Co-op"; and though all too little is known about the harbour then, we may assume that it was a jetty of wooden piles filled with blocks and rubble. It was demolished when Smeaton's Pier was built out from Castle Rock in 1770, so making way for a continuance of Wharf Road. At the inner end of Smeaton's Pier is a fisherman's shelter which was once a medieval chapel dedicated to St Leonard. It used to be served by a friar whose job it was to bless the fishermen before they put to sea. He was paid by enough of the catch for his needs. It was a productivity deal; for if he put so little into his praying that they returned to port empty-handed, Brother Friar went without his dinner! By the time the pier was built the chapel had long since fallen from grace, and was used as a blacksmith's shop for the work on the pier.

Smeaton was the illustrious engineer who had built the Eddystone Lighthouse, the one which on replacement was re-erected on Plymouth Hoe. 119 years later came the addition which acccounts for there being two lighthouses on the pier, the squat one in the middle which was where Smeaton's Pier ended, and another at the far extremity. The West Pier was constructed soon afterwards, in 1894. The stone which was brought by sea from Zennor and Carthew quarries as the most economical means of building Down'long was now to be unloaded there. That explains the crane, though it is long since I saw it used. Today, however, the West Pier is doomed to disappear beneath a massive granite building, to house the new lifeboat *Princess Royal,* which is larger than any of its predecessors and will be better placed for launching. The harbour will never look the same!

The spate of pier building occurred when there was concern, even in London, at shipping losses on the savage Atlantic coast of Devon and Cornwall. The Royal Commissioners on Harbours of Refuge sat in the town hall on 25th September 1858, taking evidence from local seafarers. Eventually they recommended that St Ives should be appointed Harbour of Refuge for the north coast of Cornwall, and that the then

princely sum of £400,000 should be allocated for the purpose. Alas, central government turned it down. In 1906 County Councillors of Devon and Cornwall joined in a deputation to Whitehall with the same end in view. That too achieved nothing, though many a stout ship was lost because, caught on a lee shore as the storm centre moved swiftly in from sea, there was no haven to which it could run for shelter. The lifeboat disaster of 1939 again highlighted the problem. Not only the hapless *Wilston* but other vessels, from which bodies were found on the beaches after that dreadful gale, would have found shelter at St Ives had the harbour been sufficiently extended. In 1939 all efforts were to be directed on the war, so still nothing was done on the scale required.

Meanwhile, back at the time of the Royal Commission, St Ives did its best on its own. The battered ruin which lies at a wide angle to Smeaton's Pier is all that remains of the "Wood" or "New" Pier built in 1864 as the first stage of an outer harbour. For the laying of the foundation stone on 30th August the town was decorated with bunting and greenery, the ceremony being followed by a regatta and by bonfires and illuminations that lit the night sky. In the evening, such was the weather in late summer that disappointingly inauspicious year, a dinner was held on the Malakoff, with the privileged of the borough and their distinguished guests wining and dining in full view of the underprivileged, like Louis XV at Versailles.

The Malakoff was a wide, open space, you know, suited to public occasions before the recent quite charming lay-out of seats and raised flower beds made it a place for relaxing in, rather than for gatherings as at the Feast Monday meet of the Western Hunt, or when it fell to my father to proclaim there King Edward VIII's accession and a few months later his abdication. 27th May 1880 was quite a day, too. In the course of an extended drought a fair was held on the Malakoff, roundabouts, fat man, the lot! On 29th all St Ives flocked there to see Bostock's famous menagerie.

How, by the way, did the Malakoff get its name? During the Crimean War (1853-6) the great Russian redoubt fired the imagination of St Ives boys. At that time, before the GWR excavated what is now the car park, the site of the Malakoff was a rocky bluff which boys at play used to charge with sticks, pretending it to be the Crimean fort. When the curved, granite retaining wall, part of the railway scheme, was raised above Pednolver Point, what name better suited such a commanding structure than that the boys had given to the rock it stood on?

The Malakoff was hewn with time-taught skills out of the everliving heart of Cornwall, as were Down'long, churches and chapels, the later piers save one and the Victorian terraces before it, and mine buildings and manor houses past and present in town and environs, and the wharf road and many sturdy houses not long after. It is part of a harmonious whole that must never be obscured by the concrete, steel and plastic of a brash new age.

The later piers save one: the Wood Pier! At the ceremonial dinner on the Malakoff in 1864 after-dinner speakers hailed the project as if Atlantic breakers never thundered upon Pendinas Head. Like the Carn Glaze pier it was timber framed. Unlike that venerable jetty it was exposed to the full fury of the gale and lasted but twenty years before bursting apart. In my youth it stretched out over the rocks resembling the skeleton of a dinosaur that had perished while negotiating the tidal arches into the harbour. Much less of it is left today. Consideration was given in the 1930s to rebuilding it as a half-tide breakwater, but nothing came of it.

These piers were necessitated during the last century not only for shelter but to accommodate the growth of the fishing industry, of coastal shipping mainly to Ireland and the Severn, and of the Mediterranean trade, which was expanding fast. To Italy with fish in Lent was an annual commitment. In 1871-2 it took fifty-three ships, no less, to carry the season's catch there. Edith Martin quotes the toast of the Pilchard Season:

"Here's health to the Pope, may he live to repent,
And add half a year to the time of his Lent,
To teach all his children from Rome to the Poles
There's nothing like Pilchards for saving their souls."

Voyages to the Black Sea such as Captain H. E. Jacobs'

brig *Mary Johns* used to make, and on which the Hain ships embarked from St Ives so long as the harbour was deep enough to float them, employed many more of our young men, and some of the old 'uns too. St Ives had become a busy little port, at a time when elsewhere West Cornwall was in despair owing to failing tin mines and the mass emigration that resulted.

When Mr W. J. Jacobs of the "Western Echo" was a very small boy his father took him to the wharf to meet an old man known as "Uncle Dal" who was near his hundredth birthday. Uncle Dal told him how, before there were Trinity House pilots to bring ships in and out of port, the job was done by "hobblers". These men were also on the look-out for vessels in distress. One morning, he said, there was a "hye and cry". A ship on fire had been sighted from the Island. Two six-oared gigs were quickly manned, Uncle Dal being coxwain of one of them. The crews stripped to the waist and competed as to which gig should reach the burning vessel first. It was not until they had rowed a few miles that they realised it must be one of those new-fangled steamers they had heard about!

The Hayle Steamship Company's SS *Herald,* a wooden paddle steamer which ran weekly to Bristol - out Wednesday, home Saturday - made her maiden voyage in September 1831. The single fare was £1.5s.0d for a cabin, 10/6 on deck (£1.25 and 52.5p.), and the trip took about twenty-two hours for the 150-mile run. The *Herald* picked up passengers from St Ives from time to time, though most ferried or forded the Hayle estuary and stayed at the Steampacket Inn awaiting embarkation. Vivian Stevens started a rival service from St Ives with his paddle steamer *Brilliant.* In 1843 the *Brilliant* raced the newest Hayle boat *Cornwall* up the Bristol Channel and reached Bristol twenty-seven minutes ahead after fourteen hours of desperate competition. It must have been a remarkable spectacle in that age of sail, those two paddle steamers thrashing past the North Cliffs with a "bone in their teeth" and the black smoke pluming over the waves!

Both companies replaced their ships with larger vessels as the years stole by. The cargo was mostly fresh produce and fish. Among the passengers were

Captain H. E. Jacobs' brig *Mary Johns* (about 1860)

The Hain Steamship *Tredenham,* launched 1915   (See pages 58 & 60.)   (Photograph courtesy P & O)

children bound for boarding school in Somerset, and up to 1859 prospective rail travellers who caught the London train at Bristol.

It was a popular run, if not always a smooth one. As is the way with the new, having at first boosted the old it did away with it. Time came when you could travel the whole way by train, a devious, not to say venturesome exercise which began at the railway station where today you make a U-turn under the viaduct at Hayle, and was no match for the sea trail the *Herald* had blazed a few years before. Eventually the Great Western Railway crossed the Tamar with the aid of Brunel and unified all the little companies in its great and still lamented organisation, and opened up the most beautiful branch line in the United Kingdom from St Erth to St Ives. So the St Ives Bay - Severn passenger run collapsed. Coastal vessels continue to ply along the north Cornwall coast and come into St Ives; but they in their turn are being driven out of business by the motorway juggernauts, while the port of Hayle shut down recently. I wonder, though, now that the earth's stock of fuel oil is dwindling, if we shall yet see the steamers again rolling a sooty plume across the bay, their bunkers full of Welsh coal from Barry; or even the graceful sailing ships spreading a cloud of canvas to the sou'westerlies as they fly for Cardiff.

Craft of every description used to be built round the harbour, where a rope walk and a net factory added to the bustle. In my childhood, though, only small boats were under construction. I remember one being launched from Tommy Thomas's boathouse between the Custom House and the Lifeboat House. A wooden baulk inset in the granite parapet opposite his workshop was lifted, and the sturdy, clinker-built boat slid over the edge of the quay and into the flood tide with a resounding splash. The Paynters were nearby competitors. Today they operate a pleasure boat service from their office under the Custom House. The last of the boat builders round the harbour was John Cothey.

Mr Laity of Ayr Manor lists larger vessels built at St Ives up to the middle of the last century. They were constructed on stocks on the harbour beach, which sloped right up to the houses before the Wharf Road

was made. The industry was captured by Harvey's of Hayle with a great deal more space for development: while waterfront extensions would have put a stop to building more such hefty craft as the *Levant Packet,* a 190-ton brig designed, as its name implies, for the Mediterranean and launched off the beach in 1828. Schooners, brigs and barques rumbled off the stocks into the teeming harbour, the last in 1855 - the *Jonadab.*

The names I chiefly recall are those of the fishing fleet. They cropped up so constantly in ordinary conversation. The *Mary Ann,* the *Rose of Sharon,* the *Brothers* - the list is inexhaustible: family names and the perpetuating of special occasions mostly. Many are recorded in a roll of honour in St Leonard's Chapel. Was it the *Mamie* which, my father said, beat off all competitors in the annual race? Which even when a rival had a new boat built in the same yard, of the same timber, to the same specifications, still won hands down? In my father's time one of the boats was named the *Stolen Revenue.* Now what dark circumstances gave rise to that? How we miss those splendid Breton crabbers sailing like great swans round the Island to anchor off the harbour. They too would race each year in the bay, and a brave sight they made.

Alas, the camaraderie of the waves is gone, although the fisherfolk of Brittany and West Cornwall throw open their doors to one another on holiday occasions. Community regulations encourage boats from fished-out waters to fish where countless generations of Cornishmen have drifted their nets. So the fish stocks will likely go the way of the pilchard shoal and herring, despite quotas less scrupulously checked in Camaret or San Sebastian than at Newlyn. Meanwhile the trawlers which have replaced the stately crabbers of our youth from time to time clash at sea with their Celtic cousins, cutting the long seine nets of the smaller Cornish boats as they compete for a diminishing haul. Local families face ruin, for nets are dear, the lost catch was their livelihood, and compensation from across the Channel is tardy.

Strangers to a town built on a narrow isthmus and surrounded by high hills may very well grasp the literal meaning of "Up'long" and "Down'long". What they fail to appreciate, sometimes after years of residence, is that these expressions are more than just indicative of direction, in the same way that "back'long" would be. Up'long and Down'long are the keys to quite different ways of life. The dividing line is the market place. Time was when almost everybody lived Down'long. Later on only the fishing community occupied the lower levels, while sea captains and professional people, the miners and the tin streamers who each worked his little stretch of the river down the Stennack, all lived higher up. Even today, when so many former fishing families have moved to the top of the Stennack, selling their homes Down'long to newcomers, it is still not easy to find common ground between the two. Until after World War One no fisherman would live Up'long, nor, for that matter, any tin miner Down'long. Neither was it the case that Up'long activists, for all that they were captains and doctors and lawyers and such, took the lead in local affairs. For generations both the constitution and the policy of the Borough Council were dictated by the fishermen's lodges on the wharf. The members of Shamrock Lodge, or the Bay View or the Rose, would sit round a red-hot stove at election time and decide how the town should vote. The candidates would court them at such times, cap - or topper - in hand, so to speak, and the arguments would continue outside the lifeboat house. I have known the fishermen return someone patently unsuitable at the top of the poll just for the fun, or the devil, of it!

Besides cottages on the wharf and various enterprises to do with fishing there were several small shops and four pubs. The White Hart became in due course Mr Laity's picturesque and fascinating tea establishment, its windows crowded with souvenirs of the Orient so that you half expected to find the shadow of a tea-clipper's top gallants athwart your hawse as you looked round. The White Hart had been built between the oldest house in St Ives and the sea. This ancient house was there before Fish Street, when Porthia was a tiny fishing village "fringing the shore", writes C. S. Murrish, "from the Castle Rocks to the foot of Skidden Hill." There were also the Ship Aground and the Globe, both shops now. Alone of the four the Sloop Inn continues to perform its hospitable function. On its walls were caricatures and portraits which artists, some of them destined to fame, had

presented to the landlord, often to "wipe the slate clean". That was largely how the art colony paid its way in early days, many a loft being hired as a studio and the rent paid in kind. My grandfather, who was architect and builder of much of St Ives in Victorian times and for twenty years after, was wont to complain, as he nailed yet another painting or photograph to the wall, that he couldn't feed his thirteen children on pictures. It used to be said, my father told me, that the back doors of all the pubs were of particular importance: without them there would have been nowhere for the abstainers to call for "a drop in the jug to cut the phlegm"!

Up to the late 1800s Fore Street was the main thoroughfare through St Ives. Short of a long detour there was no other road from the harbour. The street stretched from Chy-an-Chy, near the Mariners' Church which is now the Art Gallery, to the market place. Then as now, the Market House caused traffic problems, especially to a waggon with long spars or planks protruding astern. Next came the hard haul up Skidden Hill, which crossed what is now the top of Tregenna Hill - not a shopping centre until Victorian times - and continued right up the slope where the railings today help the uphill plodder not conditioned, as our forefathers were, to making light of the Cornish hills. Skidden Hill (formerly Skidden Lane) was so called because you had to put skids under your cart wheels on the way down; and no wonder! These skids were iron shoes chained to the cart and hooked up when not needed. From Skidden Hill the main road wound upwards by way of Talland Road, levelling out through Tregenna and then Love Lane a little below the Cornish Arms. A difficult, winding road perhaps! But there, West Cornwall had no road at all worth the name until 1703.

At the foot of Skidden Hill, Street-an-Pol leads straight to Tregenna Place. It was once called Shute Street, from an aqueduct which stood there near a pool or wall. On the site of an old house in the street, "The Retreat", is the Guildhall. It is substantially the gift of Mrs Elizabeth Noy of St Ives. She died in 1927, and her bequest was specifically for the building of a Guildhall within a stated time. Preparations had to be made within the two years of the mayoralty of my father, Alderman Percy Toy, or else the legacy would be lost to the town. They called it "Toy's Folly"! I wonder why! The foundation stone was laid in 1939 by his successor, Alderman C. W. Curnow, and the new Guildhall's offices, Court and Council Chamber, and Concert/Dance Hall are serving the town well. Previously the Borough Court sat in the Market House, while the Council met in the Passmore Edwards library.

High Street, which with the Green Court and Tregenna Hill has long since bypassed Skidden Hill, led to Squire Stephens's beautiful mansion, his town and afterwards the dower house. It was pulled down to make way for the Post Office. The Stephenses' country house was the old manor house at Ayr until they built the more pretentious and much larger Tregenna Castle in 1774.

Then Fore Street was where St Ives shopped. At Chy-an-Chy there were several bakehouses. These were where the housewives Down'long used to take their bread and splits, their pasties and their Sunday dinners, their saffron cake and buns and whatever besides for communal baking. The bakehouse provided an economical service for households which too often lived on the poverty line.

Somehow the shops in Fore Street got by despite sharing in the bad times which befall a fishing community when the catch fails. Indeed those people with a little to spare helped those without as a matter of course. That is what community is all about. "See 'ee again," the customer would remark as she left the shop without settling the bill. "See 'ee next week, my 'andsome!" It all came right in the end. There were other solutions to other problems. A grocer my father knew whose shop was at the top of the street employed a couple of apprentices. One of their tasks was to weigh out the dried fruit in the cellar. "Keep whistling, boys," you would hear him call down. "Keep whistling."

"You like your lads to enjoy their work," you observe.

"Tedn' that," he explains. "But while they'm whistling they cain't ate my currants."

A favourite establishment in my own times was Mr Armour's antique shop. It filled three floors of an ancient house which, with other buildings in St Ives, had once belonged, I believe, to the Duke of Leeds. (How far afield some of our absentee landlords lived, and how aristocratic they were!) Tales of haunting were told of it. It had a superb staircase and a painted ceiling in the Italian style, said to be done by an artist who had painted Hampton Court ceilings. The floors were crammed with a jumble of junk and valuable antiques, much of it untouched for years. It was a joy to wander round, prospecting beneath the dust, and buyers not only from St Ives but from up-country and even foreign climes picked up incredible bargains. The ground floor is now a craft shop.

Other venerable granite buildings line the street, most of them shops too. A newer, brick house, also a shop today, bears a plaque commemorating John Knill, who lived there two hundred years ago. On the wharf you can see an 18-inch-wide passage which at its inner extremity tunnels in darkness under Fore Street, straight to the house. Don't venture up it - it smells horrible. But once, they say, it smelt of brandy - smuggled. Of more recent origin are the erstwhile Primitive Methodist Chapel, now the Fore Street Methodist Church, and Zion Chapel, both at the lower end of the street. The street is cobbled for the whole of its length. How the hooves of horses clattered and iron-rimmed cartwheels rumbled, from time to time striking granite posts planted against corners to prevent damage to buildings where the thoroughfare narrowed!

Except at its Chy-an-Chy end Fore Street in John Knill's time was flanked by a row of buildings along one side only, the other side being mainly rock and sand sloping to the harbour. It ran like the gappy grin of a child, the long spaces to seaward being filled in part by sheds and ships a-building, and otherwise allowing a full view across the bay. There was no Fore Street Methodist Church. The next gap faced Knill House, from where the great man could watch the huddle of craft in the harbour and the ships billowing in from the seven seas for his inspection as Chief Customs Officer.

The Customs House, though, was not then a stone's throw distant from Custom House Steps. To get to his office Mr Knill must walk the whole length of Fore Street towards the market place, first passing a few houses opposite and a little beyond his own, then along the top of a bank known as The Cliff, clutching his cloak about him should sand and spray swirl over the cobblestones, and with scarcely a thing between himself and the sea until he came to a large house at the very top of the street. On past the church then, up St Andrew Street, and so to the Customs House at the Street-an-Pol and Skidden Hill junction above Westcott's Quay. The house was called The Gew when, on the Revenue Authority's shifting its St Ives headquarters to the foreshore, it reverted to private ownership. Now it is well renamed "The Old Customs House". The new Customs House was first a "watch house", a sturdy granite superstructure with bow windows projecting side by side and erected over an old boathouse with a fine slate floor. You can see it today just as it was, except that its splendid armorial device of later years has been deposited in the museum. It is the environment which has changed, Wharf Road stretching where the skiffs moored at its foot once jerked in the tide, while the rear façade of "Woolies" looms monstrously repulsive at its flank.

We find the new Customs House mentioned in a conveyance of property to Mr Richard Kernick Noall, along with two cottages on The Cliff, and comprising "all that Watch house Boat house and premises adjoining now in the occupation of the Commissioners for executing the Office of Lord High Admiral for the United Kingdom of Great Britain and Ireland for the use of the Coast Guard under and by virtue of a certain Indenture of Lease dated the fourteenth day of April one thousand eight hundred and sixty four." It was to be a twenty-one-year lease from 24th June 1863; and the conveyance goes on to include "all that Boat house now in the occupation of Her Majesty's Board of Customs as yearly tenants." Not that it proved possible to terminate the tenancy, yearly or not, until the Crown was ready to go - a decision that was made only recently, after the property had passed through various other hands than Mr Noall's. The Paynters' boatyard became Woolworth's, but they still occupy the boathouse.

As for the big house standing alone at the market end of Fore Street, Cyril Noall in one of his arresting newspaper articles writes that it became the Queen's Head and later on the New Inn. It is now divided into separate establishments, one of them formerly that grocer's shop where the apprentices had to whistle while weighing the currants. I am told that when the building was an inn its stable was opposite on the other side of the street. It too is a shop. The space between the inn and the sea became known as the Market Strand. My grandfather had workshops and stores there, and in 1916 the Mayor and the Member of Parliament each laid a foundation stone of the now redundant Lifeboat House, reducing Market Strand to an alleyway. Up-country folk still own many Fore Street properties but are absentees no longer, the English accent in all its variety being as common Down'long today as that of the Cornish. As for the gaps in the south side of Fore Street, even the oldest postcards and photographs show nothing of them: house and shop fronts had extended along the water's edge by the time the easels and camera tripods appeared around the quay. But you'll spot them, behind vessels beached or a-building on the foreshore, in early nineteenth century engravings.

There are several routes to the Island from the harbour. The most pleasant, save in storm time, is the walled footpath to Porthgwidden. You turn on to it below the erstwhile Seamen's Mission, now the town museum; and a rare repository of the Borough's history it is too! Other routes meander through labyrinthine streets Down'long, easily negotiated when you know how. The Island dominates the harbour. No longer an island, it obviously was once, though only the record of the rocks tells the tale. But since times unknown it has been a peninsula "sore oppressid or overcoverid with sandes", wrote Leland in 1533, "that the stormy windes and rages castith up there." On the summit of the Island stands St Nicholas's Chapel. For long a ruin, it has been carefully restored. It is floodlit, and appears to float like a golden Noah's Ark in the wastes of the night. Seafarers share St Nicholas with children, scholars and merchants as their patron saint, and the St Ives fishermen used to invoke his protection there.

Besides the ancient chapel are the even more ancient remains of prehistoric fortifications. The Cornish name of the Island, Pendinas, means the fortified headland. Nearby is a big-gun site, adjoining a coastguard station set up in 1896. Earlier batteries were manned on the Island during the interminable wars with the French.

Holinshed, the Elizabethan historian, visited these parts. He mentions that on "a little byland cape or peninsula, called Pendinas, the compass not above a mile, standeth a Pharos or light for ships that sail by those coasts in the night." This brazier-topped tower was being used as a storehouse in the 1800s, having been replaced by the lantern on a pole which Cyril Noall describes as being lit on Lamp Rock to warn ships to stand off. The lantern became redundant when Godrevy lighthouse first flashed over the Stones reef in 1859. With one recent lapse it has flashed nightly ever since, but there are doubts as to its future despite a recent reprieve from Trinity House.

On your way to the Island you may well stroll along the Digey, a narrow street leading off Fore Street. You pass on your left a quaint granite arch, the entrance to Hicks's Court. George Hicks was a famous portreeve of St Ives in 1611 and again in 1624, and while his courtyard remains, other dwellings have arisen upon the ruins of his house - pretty little places bedecked with flowers.

West of the Island is a noble stretch of sand called Porthmeor, the great beach. Atlantic rollers make it a fine beach for surfing most days of the year, but in storm times they are terrible indeed. Rocks flank the sands at either end and it was on the Island shoals that that the St Ives lifeboat finished up a battered wreck on the night of 31st January 1938, a year almost to the day before her successor too came to grief with such dreadful loss of life, as I have told. On this occasion she had taken off the crew of MV *Alba,* which had run aground in a gale. The hazardous rescue was carried out under the headlights of spectators' cars. Then the lifeboat overturned. Onlookers dragged survivors from the maelstrom, the lifeboatmen being saved but five of the *Alba* 's crew drowned. Part of the wreck remains, though you would hardly recognise it beneath its coral-like layer of limpets.

St Ives gasworks soared above this holiday beach until a German bomb demolished it in 1942. The gasometer was replaced by a huge silvery ovoid which nestled amid the houses as if just landed from outer space. This too has gone, to make way for St Ives Tate Gallery, as shall be described later. The town once supplied its own gas, very efficiently too, and at a price so low you would hardly believe it, but a German bomb put an end to that in 1942. The gasworks were opened much longer ago than you might think - in 1835; but all of 42 years had passed since a house in a nearby town, Redruth, had been the first in the world to be lit by gas. Porthmeor then had been a suitable site, the beach being almost exclusive to smugglers when the coast was clear. The initial work was carried out by Camborne men, the St Ives workers demanding a third more wages to do the job. Just before Christmas Day, only eleven years after the first steamship had appeared in the bay, and a whole generation before the lighthouse, the lamps of the town shed such a brilliance as was a wonder to behold. Great were the compliments paid to Superintendent Richards of Camborne.

But when the radiance was charged on the rates satisfaction turned to wrath, the prosecution of defaulters leading to riots. These resulted in the enlistment of a policeman for St Ives. He kept the peace, checked weights and measures, controlled juvenile exuberance, and was everybody's guide and mentor, stern but just, running his patch with tact and good humour - all on his own, all for a pound a week plus expenses. The last of St Ives' solitary policemen, Constable James Bennetts, controlled the borough from 1854 to 1889, when the County Constabulary took over. My grandfather remembered him well, speaking of him with admiration and respect and marvelliing that one man should impose his authority on such rough people in such rough times. I suppose it was because law and order was everybody's business then, and no-one passed by on the other side.

Before World War Two a local character known as "Man Friday" was the gasworks stoker. He found it a more rewardingg occupation, though, to squat on a bollard on the wharf and spin yarns to over-credulous visitors. A Midlander once enthused to me about an old salt at St Ives who had travelled the world over and held his audience spellbound with tales of faraway places. How well he had earned the half

The Digey in the '20s (Photograph by F. H. Green)

crowns and shillings pressed into his gnarled fist! This fist was Man Friday's, who had never in all his life, it was said, ventured further abroad than the Stones. He had listened avidly to mates who had sailed the seven seas, and in the days of Hain's big tramp steamer fleet with its St Ives connections there were hundreds of those. A natural aptitude for storytelling did the rest.

It is a pity that no-one was around at the time who thought of recording Man Friday's extravagances for posterity, though a restaurant on the site of his coking labours has adopted his nickname. Some of his yarns are quite original. On one occasion, it seems, he was sailing up-Channel in a full-rigged ship when a gale blew up. The captain sent every man-jack aloft to furl sail, but a sudden gust blew them all out of their sea-boots. These fell to the deck and killed the skipper, and the ship was found drifting and deserted, another mystery of the sea! Another episode I enjoyed was when a fog in the Channel "Was that thick you could lean against 'un. Which is what I did. Suddenly the fog lifted and I fell overboard."

There was a niche in society those days for eccentrics, and St Ives with its sturdy streak of individualism had its share of them. Another such was Jimmy Limpots, scion of an ancient family, Town Crier and occasional participator in nefarious activities. His lean, expressive features were beloved of artists; there are a number of drawings of him about, and they cost a pretty penny. Abe was the last of the old characters. He too was Town Crier and was painted and photographed on innumerable occasions. He took part in Town Crier competitions with considerable succcess; such a big voice from such a little, thin man! But Abe's eccentricity was not his voice, but his passion for a tidy town. For many years employed as a street sweeper, he kept St Ives spotless even when it teemed with trippers, and was not above telling a miscreant off for a dropped fag packet. Working hours meant nothing to Abe; the job was the thing. We miss him.

Nestling beneath the Island is Porthgwidden, a little beach. East of the harbour is Porthminster Beach. It was also known as Penmester, mester or minster signifying a church. There was once a village there

and an oratory, for there it was that Ia floated ashore on her leaf. In the reign of Henry VI, however, over five centuries ago, four French warships landed a raiding party. They looted the houses and then burnt them and the little church to the ground. About 1870 an exceptionally high tide swept tons of sand off the beach, and for a while the foundations of the oratory were uncovered, near the stream. Two stone coffins were found there too, with lead chalices proving monks to have been buried in them. This part of St Ives was inhabited again when cottages were built in such parts of Primrose Valley as were not occupied by beached seine boats. Larger houses, in due course guest houses and hotels, eventually replaced the lower cottages.

A feature of Porthminster Beach in my youth was the fleet of big, tarry seine boats drawn up on the foreshore and up the valley - three hundred of them, each with attendant tow-boats and bearing its owner's mark brightly coloured upon its black bows. These boats were kept solely for netting and carrying the millions of pilchards that used to swarm into the bay. They would work in threes, each group manoeuvring a quarter-mile-long net a hundred feet wide in the middle to encircle as much of the shoal as it could. There had been a race to that section of the bay which was now almost solid with fish, and millions of pilchards would be scooped by the basketful into the boats, sometimes brimming to the gunnels and half awash, and brought ashore. In the heyday of the pilchard fishery, two hundred and fifty huge seine nets were kept at St Ives, each net with its three boats to tend it, while two million pilchards a year were shipped to Italy. It was big business.

Since fishermen rowing so close to the surface could not themselves see either the extent or the perimeter of the shoal, they needed to be directed from a height. The watchers who performed this function, and without whose constant vigilance the sheen of countless scales in the bay would pass unnoticed, were called huers. They kept watch all day throughout the autumn. The steep, winding path which brings you from the beach to the top of Porthminster Hill leads you to a whitewashed shelter where today you admire the view at the beginning of the Hain Walk. This open-fronted shelter, abutting a building for storage, was the baulking (spoken of as the "bocking") house, the lookout station for the huers. When a shoal had been spotted and signalled to the beach and harbour, the cry "Hevah" (from hedva - to swarm) rang through the streets and the town emptied itself on to the foreshore. A good catch would make all the difference between prosperity and penury, bringing a fortune to the few and an end of scraping - until next season - to the many. When I was small you could often see two or three seine boats anchored offshore, the quicker to spot the hevah signals and get the fleet afloat. With tilts or covers spread they looked rather like sea-going covered waggons.

Once the boats on the beach below had been dragged down the sands to the sea, instructions were passed from above. Tin speaking trumpets were used - everyday devices when ships' officers had to shout to topmen aloft in a howling gale, and indispensable on a cliff top shouting down. Mostly, though, directions were signalled by a sort of semaphore. In earlier times the huers flourished furze bushes for the purpose, but the latest huers to occupy the hut on Porthminster Hill - this was in 1924 - waved in each hand a "bush" which was a white bag pulled over a wooden hoop with a handle. It resembled an outsized tennis racket. These bushes, with all the paraphernalia of the huers' craft, were stored in the baulking house. Remember this scene of yesteryear as you take your ease in the shelter and watch the holidaymakers stroll past.

Towards the close of Queen Elizabeth I's reign a row blew up over the attempt of a Mr Tregosse to ban the huers from his land on Porthminster Hill. This would have meant shutting off the best point of vantage in the district. Richard Hexte, gentleman, was taking similar measures against fishermen whose work required that they should trespass on his property at Tregenna Hill. Some of the trespassers were beaten up, some threatened, others taken to court. This action, which was so harmful to the wellbeing of St Ives, was met by the burgesses in council taking up the case of the Down'long people against the two powerful landlords. They sent John Tregenna, Portreeve for 1597, to London to present their plea, paying his considerable expenses of £141. This indicates the value of the huers, whose position was most affected, to the town as a whole. Mr Tregenna won the case, and St Ives gratefully returned him to Parliament as one of its two members in 1603.

Pilchards no longer swarm into St Ives Bay: the town gave up watching for them over fifty years ago. The seine boats deteriorated for want of maintenance and were at last cut up and removed. Now the herring, too, have moved on, while with the wholesale destruction of the mackerel shoals the mackerel may disappear as well. Isn't there a lesson to be learnt, somewhere?

"Millions of pilchards"   (Photographer and date unknown)

"The Primitive Methodists" by W. H. Y. Titcombe
(Photograph kindly supplied by the Dudley Art Gallery)

CHAPTER III

EVANGELISTS, TEACHERS AND ARTISTS

The Wesley brothers, John and Charles, who were both Church of England clergymen, made a great impact on St Ives. At first they were far from welcome, which in view of the puritanical streak we have already observed in the character of the town may seem surprising. An inborn dislike of change will have had a good deal to do with it. There were also political misconceptions that only time would dispel. The first visit to the district was made by Charles in 1743. By then Methodism was well established in the Midlands and the North and was moving into the South West.

Charles was the real founder of the movement. At Oxford he had assembled a group of young clerics who were resolved to apply strict rule and method to their religious observances, and called themselves Methodists. When brother John joined the coterie he became its leader. Charles was the poet of Methodism and has been hailed as the greatest hymn writer of all ages. His six and a half thousand hymns include "Jesu, lover of my soul," "Love Divine, all loves excelling" and "Hark, the Herald Angels sing". You will have heard them so often on their various occasions, and none sung with a richer blend of sweetness, harmony and fervour than in West Cornwall.

So Charles Wesley rode into St Ives. He had preached at Angarrack, thence crossing the Hayle River on horseback by "the stronde", for there was to be no causeway for another eighty-two years. A Methodist Society 120 strong had been formed in the town earlier that year, so the way was prepared for the evangelists. John arrived on 30th August, when the two brothers were met after evening service with a chanting of:

"Charles Wesley is come to town,
To try if he can pull the churches down."

Next month they preached at Zennor and sailed to Scilly in a fishing boat, but when they were back at St Ives there was violent opposition by the fishermen and miners, who broke the windows of the meeting house and smashed the seats. Some of the congregation squared up to the attackers, though the Wesleys would have turned the other cheek. Indeed, John did, after getting a clout on the side of his head, and succeeded in talking a little moderation into the ringleaders.

Charles, and sometimes John as well, used to stay at John Nance's house at the upper end of Street an Garrow (= the rough street). It was the Society's "church house" and eventually the Wesley Methodist Chapel was built right opposite. John mostly lodged with a Mr Clark in Fore Street. Both Wesleys attended the parish church on Sundays. They saw themselves as reformers rather than as founders; though John when later he began to ordain his own ministers, with which Charles disagreed, shifted his ground. At other times they preached anywhere convenient - out of doors, in private houses, or in barns, sheds and outhouses.

It was one of the latter that was the meeting house the mob pulled down to celebrate a naval victory over Spain in 1744. "Such," John bitterly observed, "is the Cornish method of thanksgiving." In fact the Cornish subscribed to the common belief, than which nothing could have been wider of the mark, that the Methodists were Jacobites who were conspiring to restore England to Roman Catholicism and Spain. John Wesley had been seen, it was averred, in France with James Stewart; he had even brought the Pretender to St Ives under the nomme de guerre of John Downes! The whole nation was at the time riddled with suspicion and mistrust, for Great Britain stood at the brink of "the '45" and Bonny Prince Charlie's bid to restore the Stewarts to the throne.

In April 1744 when John Wesley paid his second visit to St Ives, the vicar so stirred up his Easter congregation that one of Wesley's evangelists was stoned in the street. He fled for refuge to John Nance's house, which had been fortified against attack. Mr Nance and John Paynter, another leading Methodist, came to the door and were pelted with dirt.

Then chanting "Pull the house down and bring out the preacher," the mob set about forcing an entrance through the boarded-up windows. In the nick of time Mayor Stevens arrived and read the Riot Act, whereupon with "oaths and imprecations" the crowd dispersed. When the summer mission was at an end a correspondent wrote to Wesley, "The devil rages horribly."

Returning in 1745, John Wesley, preaching in Street an Garrow, was heard in silence. The Riot Act had first been read as a precaution. However, by the time that third year's visit was over the devil raged no longer. Persecution continued, though, from another quarter and was directed against the forerunners of that multitude of local preachers who were to adorn the pulpits of the Movement in years to come. The press gang moved in on several of them, while others paid the lesser penalty of imprisonment on vagrancy charges.

John Wesley's 27th and last visit to St Ives was in 1789. He preached in the market place, and just about the whole town turned up to hear.

As the years went by, the Methodists converted or built small meeting houses which come to be known as chapels. These were often demoted to Sunday Schools when replaced by the larger chapels - and some of these were very large. It is a long-forgotten fact that during service the men had to sit all together on one side of the chapel and the women on the other. Marriages could be legally held in Methodist chapels (and in registry offices) after March 1837; nevertheless most Methodists "belonged" to attend the parish church to be wed, and to be buried in the churchyard after a church funeral service. My maternal ancestors were ardent Methodists, yet they were married in Lelant church and there, in the graveyard, they lie.

During his over forty years of evangelising at St Ives, John Wesley had good reason to approve of the progress of his Movement there. The fishermen and miners, rough though they were, were converted and a generation was growing up with which he could be pleased - in every respect save one. On his eighth visit, in 1753, Wesley says of the Society, "I found an accursed thing among them. Well nigh one and all of them bought or sold smuggled goods. I told them plain that either they must put this abomination away or see my face no more. They promised to do so and I trust the plague is stayed." I cannot resist the belief, though, that even within the august ranks of the Society "the plague" outlived Wesley by many generations.

Smuggling was a way of life with the coastwise Cornish. The greatest in St Ives had a hand in it; and strangely enough one could legally buy smuggled goods. It was only the importing, distributing and selling them that broke the law. Nor, incidentally, was it only hard liquor that came from the sea as contraband. To pay for the interminable wars against the French almost every import had a sizeable duty clapped on it, a duty of which few Cornishmen approved. To reinforce his stand against smuggling John Wesley always refused to drink tea, which found its way to the "dish o' tay" in the South West as much by moonshine as under the Custom House seal.

Several large chapels were built in St Ives as Methodism spread. The most famous of these is the Fore Street Methodist Church, formerly the Primitive Methodist Chapel. Its fame is nation-, perhaps world-wide, for the pictures W. H. Y. Titcombe painted of it. Chief of these is "Primitive Methodists at Prayer". As you look at it you can almost hear the "Amens" rumbling in the throat of the ancient fisherman who kneels right up on the pew with his back to a pulpit like the bridge of a cruiser, and clasps his gnarled hands under his chin. Another old fellow below the pulpit lifts his hands in "Alleluias". The original drawing by the artist, who used local people as his models, hangs on the chapel walls alongside prints of others of his paintings. The masterpiece itself, though, is in Dudley Art Gallery.

High above the congregation, apart from a shadowy form or two in the gallery, the preacher harangues, flatters and pleads with his Lord. Quaint pearls often fell from the lips of the local preachers and their flock, whose integrity and sense of purpose did not always disguise an illiteracy that could be amusing. My father would often recount, with a twinkle in his eye, he being a churchman, how the preacher in one of the town's chapels exhorted, "Come down to we your people, O dear Lord. Come down through the roof, and we'll pay all expenses." Dr A. K. Hamilton Jenkin, who had many such tales to tell, described how a local preacher began his sermon with, "In my Father's house are many mansions." Before he could plunge into his diatribe, a member of the congregation roared out indignantly (and I cannot but quote Dr Jenkin word for word), "'Tes nothen' more than a great strammin' lie what thee'rt telling. We do all knaw well enough that your father's house haven't got but three rooms in it - and one of them's no bigger than a pig's crow (sty)." Another of his stories concerns a fisherman who lay at death's door. His brother bent over him. "Goodbye, Jan booy," he murmured. "Tell fayther when you do see him that the Meary Jane have been lengthened ten feet by the starn. He'll be glad to knaw." "Mikey Noon-a" was a local character my father knew who, repenting of a misspent life, joined the Salvation Army and was entrusted with the bass drum. Called upon one hapless Sabbath to testify, Noon-a boomed in a voice that rang throughout the wharf, "I was a sinner and a drunkard. But following the Lord I'm that darned happy I could put my fist right through this bloody drum!"

Fore Street Chapel was constructed in 1837, much of it from blue elvan "bowlies" brought by boat from Porthmeor. These bowlies are those large stones rounded and smoothed by the everlasting grinding of the tides. When each boat arrived in the harbour the Down'long women carried the stones to the site of the new chapel in their aprons.

Chapel catered for the Cornishman's natural aptitude for music, recognising it as an indispensable supplement to the gospel teaching, and a source of satisfaction and comfort to many. Congregational singing, everybody joining in without inhibition and harmonising because born to it, was splendid to hear and inspiring to take part in. It still is. Each chapel boasted a fine choir, and in addition to Sunday services presented services of songs and oratorios too, sometimes importing well-known soloists. Mr Ernest White, a St Ives baritone and a musician of distinction, is well remembered for producing these admirable performances.

Indeed, a great deal of the social life of St Ives revolved round church and chapel when I was a girl, as it had done throughout the previous century. Services and music, and also teas and suppers, sewing meetings and concerts and outings relieved winter evenings, filled limited hours of leisure, and offered something to look forward to during the long working week. For the children there was Sunday School, with its annual bonus when the children paraded through the town with their school banner, and sometimes a brass band, to where the "bun fight" was to be held. This was in fact no battle ground, save insofar as there was breathless competition in running and jumping, and games; all followed by tea from an enormous urn and a saffron bun as big as a plate. The tea treat ended with everyone worn out, children and adults alike, and already looking forward to the next red-letter day a year hence. Such simple pursuits might hardly be understood as pleasurable today, but we enjoyed them.

A different brand of evangelism came to St Ives in 1861 and '62, when the forerunners of "God's Army" paraded in the streets. For Rev. William Booth, later General and founder of the Salvation Army, was leading a two-year mission to the Borough. His campaign was conducted from the Wesley Chapel in the Stennack, and the St Ives Corps was established seventeen years afterwards. In 1936 Evangeline Booth, herself then General of the "Army", unveiled before a huge audience a plaque commemorating her father's mission. You can see it on the walls of the Citadel on the wharf, next to the lifeboat house. The Salvation Army celebrated its St Ives centenary in July 1979.

St Ives, like all seaports, has always held the "Sally Allee" in warm regard. Wherever the "exigencies of the service" took a seaman - and the tally of St Ives seamen is prodigious - there was the Salvation Army to turn to for shelter and comfort, no questions asked. How many of our naval lads in two world wars found respite there from a huddle of hammocks and overcrowded messdecks! How often they got practical help when they themselves were not free to sort out the problems of home! Not for nothing did the Citadel adjoin the lifeboat house. The lifeboat would return from battling with the gale, and there was the Salvation Army ready for the rescued crew with blankets and hot drinks and somewhere to lie snug until the nightmare of shipwreck had been exorcised in

General Evangeline Booth commemorates the 75th Anniversary of
Salvation Army Founder William Booth's mission to St Ives.
Alderman W. P. Toy, J. P., Mayor of St Ives

sleep.

It was this comforting, this homeliness that marked the Salvationist movement as different from any other. They prepared a man for religion by first caring for him. Then they brought God into his home, if he had one, and gave him a temporary home with God in it, if he hadn't. Salvation came into the cottage through every possible doorway; even by the sale, at knock-down prices, of rugs and quilts tapestried with texts, and of pictures that a man who had found God might care to display.

The musical side of the "Army" is of special appeal to the Cornish, whose love of song is equalled by their love of brass bands. In my home at Carbis Bay I have often listened enraptured as the strains of the Salvation Army band, and the joyous singing on the wharf by thousands of St Ives folk and their visitors of hymns best loved by saved and sinner alike, wafted across the bay of a summer Sunday evening. It is an experience "quite out of this world", as they say. You may have heard it on radio or TV, from St Ives or from other Cornish harbours. General Booth once asked, "Why should the devil have all the best tunes?" Thanks to God's Army, he doesn't!

At the top of Tregenna Hill you will see the Catholic Church of late Victorian construction. A small chemist's shop used to stand on the site, and was favoured by the well-to-do residents of Sir Christopher Hawkins' Terrace. This is now just "The Terrace". The main thoroughfare in front of it was then private, gated at either end.

Sunday Schools originally offered basic as well as religious education to poorer youngsters who could not afford the fees of the town's private schools. Then came the Wesley Day School in the big schoolroom built on to the chapel at the bottom of the Stennack in 1845. Terms were tuppence a week for the under-sixes and threepence for the over-sixes. The National Church of England School followed a couple of years afterwards, was improved in '68, and closed down in 1925, its main schoolroom becoming the parish room. The Board School in the Stennack was opened in 1881. It became St Ives Junior School, and a fine building it is too. We Cornish delight in granite. My father-in-law, Mr C. H. Bray, when headmaster inaugurated rugby football in Cornish schools - it was all soccer till then - and had the satisfaction of seeing two of his pupils, Roach and Gyles, sporting the white shirt with the red rose of English schoolboy internationals. With post-war reorganisation the school was moved to Trenwith, and now the old school is St Ives NHS surgery.

The first school in St Ives has been mentioned already. It was the Free Grammar School granted under the charter of 1639 but not opened until the Commonwealth. It fades out of the records in 1672. St Christopher's School in the Belyars used to be the worthy successor of a long line of private and dames' schools. Alas, it is no more! It disrupted, to move to Carbis Bay as St Eia's. In my father's early days there were two excellent private schools Down'long, both masters having the identical name. One was therefore known as Mr James Teapot Rowe and the other was Mr James Sugar-basin Rowe. The reason for this nomenclature has never been explained to me. Strangely enough it in no way detracted from the respect with which these two schoolmasters were held in the town.

Teapot Rowe's school in Court Cocking lost too many pupils to the new Board School and closed down when my father was an infant. Sugar-basin Rowe's, in Academy Place, saw the century out, though the old gentleman himself died in 1896. My grandfather, a churchwarden and prominent Anglican in St Ives, sent his two elder sons to the National School. However, an overdose of raps on the knuckle inspired my father to hurl his slate at the headmaster, whereupon my grandfather saw fit to remove both his boys and send them to Mr Rowe's in Academy Place. Many of the town's leading personalities were taught there, and well taught too. Discipline was firm, as always in Victorian times, and I never knew my father to criticise it. He told with amusement of two of his schoolmates who "got away with it", though. These two, brothers, were strictly brought up never to drink anything stronger than water. However, this abstemiousness had not held them from the tobacco habit at an early age - chewing of course, otherwise they would have been found out. They kept a tin in their desk into which to squirt the juice in class time, behind the raised lid, with the accuracy chewers of the quid acquired before the stickier, if less volatile, invention of chewing gum.

The GWR branch line, which came into service in 1877, introduced to the town newcomers who brought it a far wider fame than it had previously known and, no doubt fortuitously, an industry which was to replace its declining traditional occupations. St Ives, though, was not readily to move out of age-long isolation, nor to abandon its admirable intention to do its own thing in its own way, nor to reject its suspicion of strangers. When my father was a small boy the children would follow a stranger through the streets. But the Great Western Railway had absorbed the minor companies and was speeding English foreigners into the Duchy over the Brunel bridge, among them artists seeking inspiration in the now easily accessible solitudes of the Cornish. The train da-diddley-dumped them, as trains used to, down seventy miles of Cornwall, mysterious land of Arthur and, as was then supposed, of Druids, much of it scarred by mining already in decay yet still not mellowed by the green fingers of time nor the romance of ivied ruins. A few pioneers stepped off on to the St Ives line at St Erth - and into wonderland.

Meandering along the coast through Lelant and Carbis Bay they marvelled - and haven't we all? - at the scenic beauty of St Ives Bay. The artistic eye discovered such a range of colour as it had not seen elsewhere than in the Bay of Naples, and detected that quality in the light which was mirrored from the white sandy sea-bed and was to be captured in their brushes. In the harbour they found an irresistible theme for their work. The word went round at Chelsea, and in St Ives sail lofts became studios. Easels appeared among the bollards and nets and crab pots on the wharf. By 1885 an Art Colony had taken root, the Newlyn Colony just beating St Ives to it. Early on the scene were Whistler and Sickert. Mr and Mrs Harwood Robinson turned up and settled. Louis and Wyly Grier, Adrian Stokes, Julius Olsson, Titcombe painter of fisherfolk, whose work we have already admired in the Fore Street Chapel, and numerous other artists of repute followed down the line. The art galleries of England, and then of Europe and America, showed St Ives to the world.

The artists as a body, however popular individuals among them became, were not at first welcome, and I doubt whether they were ever assimilated Down'long, even though so many lived there and painted around the harbour. They were rather too free-thinking for the "locals". The story is still told of the artist who persisted in painting on the wharf on a Sunday. The fishermen threw his canvas into the harbour, then his easel, and lastly himself.

Lanham's opened a gallery in 1887 for exhibiting the pictures of the growing Art Colony. It still presents an impressive show of St Ives art. A year later Louis Grier founded the Arts Club; it is the old, black, part-timber building on Westcott's Quay and measures its ninety-plus years of existence in tide and tempest, and an uninterrupted succession of lectures and plays and concerts all to the critical standards of its membership. This includes many illustrious names.

In 1927 came the St Ives Society of Artists, who twenty years later established their own art gallery in the Mariners' Church. This massive granite structure behind the Sloop was built by my grandfather when the car park there was the site of houses so huddled together that many of their rooms lacked windows. It had been erected in the early 1900s in memory of a beloved Vicar of St Ives, Canon Jones; and when the foundations were dug the ruins of very old houses came to light, "overcoverid with sandes" as Leland had written in Henry VIII's days. Congregations shrank and the most recent denizens of Down'long - with some Up'longers besides - have made creative, attractive use of it.

Time came when the devotees of later art forms considered that a society of traditionalists offered them too little scope. A leading member, Commander Roskruge, supported them and the Penwith Society of Arts opened its own gallery in a one-time fish cellar in Porthmeor Road.

Now we have moved on. The St Ives Tate Gallery, due to be opened in Spring 1993, already dominates the Porthmeor sea-front. Designed by the two architects of the new Truro law courts, it is itself of consequence in the art world. With whatever qualms neighbouring residents endured its construction in so constricted a

Above: The Mariners' Church, St Ives, built by Lena's grandfather and now used as an art gallery
Below: Work in progress on the St Ives Tate Gallery, September 1992   (Photograph by Bob Acton)

45

space, they can view with pride the noble edifice that covers the gasworks site, occupied for half a century by the bizarre silvery container we had grown accustomed to but never much cared for. Hitler's bomb destroyed it. So now, where Man Friday, teller of tall tales, once dossed down on the coke, a Temple of Art is to exhibit masterpieces by artists who pioneered at St Ives the avant-garde art of the post-war generation.

The gallery, provided and owned by Cornwall County Council (which sadly classifies it as a "museum") is managed by the London Tate. We are to see there paintings, sculptures, drawings, prints and ceramics by artists who lived and worked among us from 1925 to 1975 - the year of Dame Barbara Hepworth's death. Large numbers of their works shown and stored at the London Tate are to be transferred to St Ives, forty or fifty to be exchanged from time to time between the two galleries.

The roll of famous artists, charmed by the clear light and bright waters of St Ives Bay, which they likened to the Bay of Naples, is formidable. It will grow - unless the Water Company's insistence on discharging Mounts Bay waste into our lovely bay proves as disastrous, despite purification schemes, as those of us fear who know our tides and currents, and the pounding of the nor'-easter over the Stones. Some whom we would watch at work between Clodgy and Hawkes Point, when easels were "as plentiful as tabby cats", or meet in their studios on Open Day, were prior to the Tate's deadline. Of the moderns who will surely have their niche in the Tate we have visited Patrick Heron busy in his eyrie at Eagle's Nest, Zennor, where he surveys the straits of sky and sea and moorland. We knew Peter Lanyon as a boy at The Red House, he who like Icarus soared, to view from his glider what he would paint, and like Icarus crashed. We saw Alfred Wallis, the inspiration we are told of Ben Nicholson, with his paint pots and boards and pieces of cardboard that were his canvases, and also on his rag-and-bone rounds. Wallis's talents were perceived in the '20s and are the admiration of the artistic community today.

As youngsters we tried our hand at Bernard Leach's pottery on top of the Stennack; it was the recipient of Hitler's second bomb on St Ives, but rose from the ashes. Dame Barbara Hepworth and Ben Nicholson came to Carbis Bay before they settled in St Ives. Her huge concrete abstractions used to be displayed in what had been my grandfather's garden, beside Bedford Road Chapel. The old cinema-cum-palais-de-danse at the foot of Barnoon Hill became her studio, and the great lady perished in a fire there, as perhaps you will remember. Her sculptures are to be found the world over. I have seen them as far overseas as New Zealand and Australia. One of them stands on the Malakoff, others in Trewyn gardens and the forecourt of the Guildhall. Universally approved though they are, they are not always understood. Confessing as much to a fisherman who, like me, was viewing the Guildhall masterpiece for the first time, I was duly enlightened. "Don't 'ee knaw what 'tes, then? 'Tes an old problem solved at last, putting a round hole in a square peg." Like all wit, it bears the bite of truth!

With the new Tate committed to fifty years of experiment, change and challenge in the world of Art, yet may it never ignore the great founders of the St Ives Colony when faithfulness to its subject was a virtue in a painting, and understanding more gratifying than enigma to a viewer.

The railway brought the artist, the artist sketched and photographed and wrote, and the visitor got the message and came. At first the most distinguished participants in the world scene arrived, in search of rest and change and fresh air. You could see them on the pier of a summer's day - Prime Ministers and Cabinet Ministers and Potentates and their ladies, and the merely rich, dropping a word or two to a community that was more critical than they realised but too polite to say so. I have seen both Crown Prince Chichibu of Japan and Herr Ribbentrop, Hitler's foreign secretary, at Tregenna Castle, though on separate occasions. It was said later that the Castle was to have been Ribbentrop's share of the loot when the Nazis took over in Britain.

The war over, travel ceased to be the privilege of the few and all roads led sou'west. Cornwall became the leisure-land of the nation, with St Ives most desirable among the resorts. There is something excitingly foreign about St Ives. As you join the colourful throng Down'long in "the Season" you feel you are no longer in England. And neither are you, you know!

The West Pier and Pedn Olva, St Ives, in the 1920s (F. H. Green)

This view, looking up Tregenna Hill from Tregenna Place,
shows the aftermath of the flood of 1894.

CHAPTER IV

MAINLY UP'LONG

The forces of nature struck three mighty blows in the early 1890s. First was the great blizzard of '91. It wreaked havoc throughout the South West. St Ives was spared the worst of it, though isolated for a time by snowdrifts, while the inhabitants plundered the new pier, already disintegrating, for firewood. '93 witnessed the *Cintra* Gale, which cast four steamships ashore in St Ives Bay in one November day and swallowed up a fifth, as told in Chapter VII. In '94 came the flood.

There had been continuous downpour on the hills above St Ives - November again! - and on the 12th the accumulated water burst into the streets. "The torrent, coming down the Terrace main road," wrote an eye-witness, "quickly filled the Malakoff, and, bursting the walls, poured into the Railway Yard, rushed past the Station and over the embankment into the sea." Far worse than that it cascaded down the Stennack, where waves mounted to six feet high in Chapel Street, and swept through the town all of the November day. The flood carried great rocks and stones along with it into the lower streets, whole houses being washed away. More commonly the water rushed in at one door and out at another, "knocking out walls and carrying away furniture." Gas and water mains were destroyed, with damage to property that has never been assessed. But not a single life was lost; though had the hills disgorged their vengeance at night, who knows what the tally of dead might have been?

A stream has always flowed down the Stennack, though you would not guess it today, for it has been piped underground as the Stennack was built up. Long ago the Stennack was but a valley through which a road skirted fields and orchards and cottages, while behind the present Western Hotel the stream worked a couple of grist, or corn, mills. The road winds uphill. It was known as the country road out of St Ives and meets the ancient "West Way" to Penzance via Lelant. This is now spoken of as the Old Coach Road, though with

what justification I do not know.

The word Stennack means "the place of tin", and this sums up most of the activity in the valley when tin was booming, off and on, through much of the nineteenth century. Streamers were at work in the Stennack River. Each group, often working in pairs, dug and shovelled and sifted the grains of black tin, or tinstone, washed down from the high moors, and scraped a living out of it. For the grains among the sand and silt might be few, but they were 65% pure tin. It was hard work but healthy, with none of the ills that beset the miner underground, and according to Dr Hamilton Jenkin accounted for the broad shoulders which made a Cornish battalion drawn up in line occupy more space than any other.

The homes of the tinners - the miners and the streamers - were Up'long in the Stennack. They would no more have lived Down'long than the fisherfolk would then have moved Up'long. Many of the miners worked at the Trenwith mine, half-way up the Stennack; its count house stands in Trenwith burrows. Mining was a job which used to employ whole families, caught in the cogs, as it were, of the Industrial Revolution. Life was hard for the cottager, and never more so than when his work took him underground, and his children too, a thousand and more feet down where the lodes of ore awaited his strength and skill, and exacted the dread toll of crystal-sharp rock dust in his lungs: when his wife too laboured in the surface workings, and the livelihood of the family depended on the national demand for tin and copper. But he took pride in his job, and was satisfied that in good times his earnings outclassed those of agricultural labourers, and that he was nobody's man but his own.

Trenwith was mainly a coppermine, though a little tin was raised there as well. Came the depression, when it closed, but a new company took over in 1908, and mostly working the dumps produced about seven hundred tons of uranium ore in the next nine years. This was how Mr W. J. Jacobs describes the venture in his journal: "When Trenwith mine was opened a quantity of radio-active material was recovered. The concentrates were sent to Sir William Ramsay, a celebrated scientist of the time, who collaborated with Mme Curie, the famous French scientist. The Directors of the mine were named Schiff, and one of them wished to give a demonstration to his friends in the St Ives district of the newly discovered substance called radium. He borrowed the Masonic Hall for the purpose and I was one of the selected audience. After giving an interesting discourse on the possible uses of radium, Mr Schiff asked if any man present would lend him a metal cigarette case. This was soon forthcoming and Mr Schiff put a small phial of radium inside the cigarette case. He then asked that the Hall lights be extinguished. The cigarette case was placed on the table and we were left in darkness. After three or four minutes we saw a gradual glow coming from the table. He then asked that the lights be re-lit and we saw the radium had penetrated the cigarette case. Afterwards we heard that this phial of radium had been sent to the German University of Charlottenburg."

Higher up the Stennack, and on the same left hand side as the mine, was Trenwith village, swallowed up in St Ives as the town spread into the hills. The Trenwith family, who had lived in the manor house there for many generations, died out in the mid-1700s. Then a distant relative named Lander turned up in Plymouth and inherited the manor, which he sold off piecemeal. Much of the Trenwith manor house has defied decay and hard dealings, and is now occupied by another St Ives family.

Top right of the Stennack is Hellesvean hamlet, home of the late Richard John Noall, who discovered the remains of a "Dark Ages" home there. This ardent Cornishman and antiquary is affectionately remembered by many of us still. He was an inspiration to all who desired to know this little seaport as it was when our forefathers trod its ancient streets. Richard John told me of a couple who lived at Hellesvean with their only child, a strapping young man whose chore it was to draw the family water at the well. One day he failed to return home at the usual time so the parents,

becoming worried, went out in search of him. All they found were signs of a struggle and his broken pitcher at the well; but looking over the bay they saw a ship of the Royal Navy standing out to sea. The pressgang had landed, and their son had been taken.

Months later as the old couple sat in the kitchen, with the upper half of the "hep" door hooked back to admit the sunshine, a shared impulse turned their gaze to the door. In the open "hep", smiling at them, stood their lost boy. With cries of welcome they sprang to their feet, flung the whole door wide, and - no one was there! Both had seen him, had warmed to his smile - and he was not there. Trembling, his arms about the sobbing mother, the old man glanced at the calendar above the mantelshelf. The first day of June, 1794. A day of omen! What could this vision portend?

A few weeks later they knew. A letter from the fleet regretted that their gallant son had died in victorious action against the French in mid-Atlantic. The battle is known as the Glorious First of June.

Now you can spot the queer tower of St John's in the Fields, the parish church of Halsetown, but where have all the green fields gone? Inaugurated in 1846 the church is the work of the architect J. P. St Aubyn. The Poet Laureate, John Betjeman, describes it as "The gaunt slate and granite church of St John....with lean-to aisles, high nave with ingenious wooden roof, and lit by a clerestory." The 66-foot-high tower has a gabled roof. Within, an open-plan effect: centred altar, huge carpet, no pews. Not what you expect of a Victorian church, but I like it! On an interior wall is a recent memorial tablet to Rev. T. C. Barfett, vicar for 54 years, and his wife. It was carved in oak by Rev. John Harvey, whose masterpieces of woodcraft adorn many Cornish homes and churches, Truro Cathedral among them, and are known even in Australia. Before taking holy orders as a young man, "John Willie" was a master at the Stennack school.

Past Hellesvean the road forks. One fork leads on up the hill to Zennor, St Just and Lands End. The other turns left at Consols mine past Hellesveor Chapel to Halsetown and the reservoir. Consols was one of many mines that ringed St Ives. Taking them anti-clockwise you start within the town, on Pednolver Point at the end of the Warren. There Pednolver mine dominated Porthminster Beach. Where my father remembered an engine house and a cottage, the hotel of that name now stands. There were tin mines even where you would hardly credit there was space for them, but of course 90% was out of sight. Wheal Dream was where the Town Museum is sited. Wheal Snuff on the Island overlooked Porthmeor Beach; nearby are traces of incredibly ancient open workings. Records indicate two other Island mines. Wheal Ayr flourished in the neighbourhood of the Stephenses' country house and estate before they moved to Tregenna Castle. Ayr engine house was converted into an intriguing dwelling and lived in for years before being demolished to make way for a garage. Then came Consols and a host of mines right round to Wheal Margery on Porthminster Point above Carbis Bay Beach. The stacks and romantic looking ruins you see on Rosewall Hill are all that is left of the Rosewall Hill and Ransom United Mine.

The Account House of St Ives Consols mine has become a farmhouse. My grandfather Robert Toy (it is one of several 17th century Huguenot names in Cornwall) used to turn his carthorses out to grass either there at Consols or at "Little in Sight" opposite Trenwith Burrows. They would be driven to the granite quarries around - Balnoon and Towednack mostly - and haul the stone to the site for the masons to cut on the job. It often fell to my father and his elder brother, as boys, to tumble out of their bed before dawn in their home at the Elms - Bedford Road Chapel was not its neighbour then - to round up the team for the day's work. Grandfather is ever present to me in the fine granite buildings, mainly at St Ives but also as far afield as Penzance and Newquay, which he built and usually planned too. Besides the Mariners' Church Down'long and Barclays Bank, he gave shape and substance to acres of detached houses and terraces Up'long. At the time prefabricated window frames and such were unknown, at St Ives anyhow. Made to measure in his Market Strand workshop, they are lasting well. It was in the closing days of self-sufficiency, a receding source of superior craftsmanship and regular employment. When he died in 1928, sixteen years after retiring, his obituary notice stated, "To him belongs the credit of having the foresight to commence the opening up of our old

fishing town so that it should become a residential town.... He was one of the pioneers in the development of St Ives."

On Consols pond, where you turn left off the Zennor road for either Nancledra or the West Way, the boys of the town - and "old boys" too - sail model yachts every Good Friday. An alternative spot was the pool in the sand at the foot of the West Pier. The event dates from antiquity, when at the start of the summer fishermen would send miniature craft out into the Bay as an offering to the gods of the Cornish seas, to buy therewith safety for themselves and their boats when out fishing.

And so on to Halsetown, bearing in mind that in Cornwall the term "town" frequently implies no more than a village. Mr Halse's town was the first in Great Britain - the first in the world for all I know, the ancient civilisations excepted - to be town-planned. He built the cottages for the tin and copper miners in the neighbourhood. They stood in pairs instead of in terraces, each with a garden large enough to sustain a family. He also gave his village a school and a house for the schoolmaster.

James Halse was born in Truro in 1769. He was a descendant of the De Als, later Hals, of St Buryan, who for a time held the Trembethow estate near Trencrom. An oft-quoted Hals is the seventeenth-century Cornish historian. Our Mr Halse, a solicitor, settled in the district when he was twenty-one and in turn became our Town Clerk, Deputy Recorder and twice Mayor of St Ives. At first he lived next door to Halsetown Inn. His house is surprisingly roomy inside and has beautiful door mouldings, as in his St Ives residence. This he built in 1820; it is now Messrs Chellew's offices in Fernlea Terrace. Because it then stood in a field with no access roads, everybody called it "Halse's Folly", but a road was soon skirting the front door. Halse had moved from the village to St Ives because he planned to contest one of the Borough's two parliamentary seats and a St Ives address was necessary. In the event he beat the poet Mackworth Praed of Trevethoe in the General Election of 1826 and sat in five parliaments, three of them as sole Member for St Ives after the reforms of 1832. Another Praed won the seat after all, at a by-election when

James Halse's house, St Ives

James Halse, philanthropist and great friend of the town, died in 1838.

Whereas James Halse, Esq., MP, will ever be honoured in St Ives, the whole western world honoured another man associated with Halsetown and born the very year of its founder's death. It came about like this. A Mr Samuel Brodribb, whom his own grandson was to describe as "lured by a lively and inquisitive interest in almost anything but his work", was a travelling salesman from Somerset. A Mr Behenna, a Falmouth man of a comparable aversion and with a wife of exceptional beauty, had acquired Boskerris Woolas and Boskerris Wartha Farms at Carbis Bay through the good offices, and maybe a little persuasion somewhere along the line, of the squire. He had two comely daughters, Mary and Sarah. Sarah married Isaac Penberthy, a Halsetown mine captain, while her sister fell for Sam Brodribb, who wooed her during a desultory sales tour of the far South West and wed her, bearing her off to Bristol.

There they had a son, John Henry; and it was to Sarah that Mary, driven to a precarious livelihood, decided to send her infant son rather than attempt to rear him in urban squalor. So despite Sam's protests Mary Brodribb packed off the child to his aunt and great Viking of an uncle, who managed four tin mines in the Halsetown area. There Johnny was for six years a happy member of the Cornish family, admiring and a bit in awe of Cousin John, adored by Cousin Kitty, taking the lead in dressing-up games and pranks, and brought up in love and devotion by Aunt Sarah, who was a pillar of the chapel.

Once a year mother turned up at the Halsetown house - it is the square, granite building at the bend of the road opposite the pub - to take him home to father in Bristol for a short stay. They would travel adventurously by the little paddle steamer *Brilliant*, already referred to as plying between St Ives and Bristol.

Having learnt to read and write at Halsetown school, Johnny devoured the only books in the Penberthy household - the Bible, *Don Quixote* and an anthology of ballads. To these Shakespeare came to be added, together with the make-believe of Cornish guise-dancing (of which more later), fairs and circuses, and amateur melodrama by Mr Crink of Carbis Bay. And ultimately - O glorious climax! - professional Shakespeare at St Ives.

Now Henry John Brodribb begins to take over. A picnic party bound for Carbis Bay Beach shelters from the rain in a wayside cottage. A ten-year-old, J. H. no less, regales his companions with a startling demonstration of ventriloquism. The news spreads and Aunt Sarah's heart-searchings become acute. Methodist as she is, acting is a sin. Yet here is her beloved nephew all set for the stage, though as devout a Christian as herself. He goes to London, changes his name, and becomes at eighteen Henry, and at fifty-seven *Sir* Henry Irving, Supremo of the Victorian footlights, the first actor ever to receive the accolade.

When you leave Halsetown and just before you get to Giew Mine, the last mine to have been active in the St Ives district, you can either continue straight on through Nancledra for Penzance or else turn along the West Way to join the spine road through the county. Some of my mother's people farmed land on the seaward side of the West Way during the eighteenth and nineteenth centuries, and perhaps in the previous centuries too. For their farmhouse, Westaway, was a medieval building and when they abandoned it I would guess it had been little enough modernised. They moved into Carbis Bay in the late 1800s and the farmhouse fell into ruin, being now but a heap of rubble with nettles and brambles writhing over the fallen stones and the slate slabs of the roof. In the talfet, my mother told me - she knew the old place well - a crucifix was found. Did it betoken furtive revivals of Catholicism after the Prayer Book Rebellion, when the Portreeve was executed? Was it late in Elizabeth's reign that a hunted man hid there, when every Catholic was presumed a conspirator against Queen and Realm? Or had an emissary of "The King over the water" skulked in that chamber constructed half-way over the living room and boarded at the end to give privacy? Whenever it was that Westaway displayed Christ Crucified on the beams of the talfet, the building was remote enough for secrecy, where its remains are still hard to find. As for the descendants of the family there, they were all as staunch Methodists as their relations at Carbis Bay, long before my grandfather moved to the coast. But once, maybe, the family had spoken the louder to drown the creaking of floorboards in the half-loft above while they entertained the Lord Protector's officer, or the Queen's, or the German King's!

By "Westa" is Liza's Pool. Though now overgrown with trees and bushes the water glints there still and is reputed to be bottomless. Liza was some unfortunate girl who drowned herself for love in its black depths; and if spectres haunt Westaway who can wonder? Not that I have heard mention of any.

Trevarrack Valley meanders down between Trencrom and Trink Hills to south'ard and Worvas Hill to the north. At Trevarrack hamlet it passes a great, grey granite boulder mottled with lichen. This boulder, no less an authority than the National Trust informs you, was used by the Giant of Trencrom when playing bowls. Thus it will hardly surprise you that it is called Bowl Rock. But should you find the name unconvincing as to the facts, you may prefer another explanation of this isolated lump of rock. Giant Cormoran of St Michael's Mount and his opposite number on Trecrobben, or Trencrom, Hill used to play games which involved hurling or skimming stones in friendly, and sometimes far from friendly, rivalry. Bowl Rock is one that missed! Be that as it may John Wesley, who though short of stature chose to stand high when conducting a service, stood on Bowl Rock to preach to the miners and countryfolk who flocked down the West Way to listen and to sing with him his brother Charles's hymns. Trevarrack is well named "the homestead by the rock". An old Wesleyan chapel is on the opposite side of the road and reached by a stile and a little lane. Lurking among the trees nearby is the former Trevarrack School, now a pub named the Tyringham Arms after the last squire. Like so many of our Cornish Board schools it is a most pleasing building of warm granite. Down now between hedges of rhododendrons past St Ives Holiday Village, very much a creation of the late 1900s, and so to the main gates and lodge of Trevethoe, home of squires Praed, Mackworth and finally Tyringham until the Tempests took it over for their photographic business. There the West Way ends.

The ridge which separates you from the town as you follow the West Way dominates the Ancient Borough. On its seaward side sprawls·Tregenna Castle, once the residence of the Stephenses but throughout this present century a hotel. Although much has been added to the original manor house Squire Samuel Stephens would still recognise his own home. It lies in Tregenna Woods; and above the trees, on rhododendron- and fir-crowned Worvas Hill into which each successive developer hacks a further swathe, Knill's Steeple stabs into the sky. Standing at its base you can see both St Ives Bay and Mount's Bay at a turn of the head. This steeple, or if you prefer this monument, obelisk or mausoleum, for it has nothing to do with a church, was built as his own tomb by John Knill, whose house you saw in Fore Street. However, the coffin chamber, which is exposed every fifth year according to the terms of his extraordinary will, is empty.

As it was when in 1801 the first Knill's celebrations took place, John Knill having ten years yet to live. It was to stay empty because of difficulties in getting the ground at the Steeple consecrated. In his Last Will and Testament this Mayor and Collector of Customs at St Ives, the privateer owner and smuggler and eventual magistrate of Middlesex, bequeathed his body to the dissectionists and required its burial near his London home. Another side of this most colourful of the many colourful characters in our borough's long story was shown in his enthusiasm for Freemasonry. He was a founder member of St Ives' first masonic lodge, the Ship Lodge (No. 240), sixth of the Cornish lodges. It was founded on 16th July 1765 and first met at the Ship Inn "long since demolished for highway improvement". John Knill was elected to the Chair and the landlord, Nathaniel Hicks, was Treasurer. There is doubt as to where the Ship Inn was.

1772 to '77 were troublesome years. Mr Hicks died and with the inn under new management alternative accommodation had to be found. This was eventually arranged at the Queen's Head, at the church end of Fore Street, and a flourish of activity followed. But "1779 was a trying year." (I quote from a lecture on the Lodge history.) "Four successive meetings were abandoned in August and September by reason of the alarm given to the coast by the combined fleets of France and Spain, which threatened invasion." The

Ship Lodge endured only to 1781, largely because of the reluctance of Mr Knill and his intimates to share office wiith his brethren. Noble items of lodge furniture, presented by Sir John St Aubyn, now embellish the Masonic Hall at Hayle.

On 15th March 1870 Freemasonry was revived at St Ives. The members were to meet at premises under construction in Fore Street, though in fact their present and permanent headquarters came to be in St Andrew's Street. A senior officer of the new Tregenna Lodge was mine host of the White Hart Inn, and here the brethren adjourned for repasts described as both "sumptuous" and "bountiful". Mr J. Laity discovered a masonic window in the premises when, the White Hart having closed its dooors, he opened his shop there.

But back to the mausoleum on Worvas Hill! By the time Mr Knill was interred, not there but at Holborn, the celebrations attendant on the administration had twice been enacted, though on neither occasion had he witnessed the ceremony. Whoever is in St Ives on 25th July (or if a Sunday, the 26th) of every fifth year since 1801 may witness the quinquennial procession from Market Place to Steeple, and if in good trim, for it is a long, stiff climb, tag on at the end. The Steeple is a slender, three-sided pyramid built of granite on a high base and bearing the Knill coat of arms with the prophetic motto "Resurgam" - I shall rise again. Far away though John Knill lies you can sense his presence - a kindly, comfortable presence - on this Cornish hilltop where there is little to disturb the silences of the moors but the moan of the wind and gulls. The mausoleum is visible for miles around and is a prominent landmark for ships at sea. Some say it was erected not so much to receive Mr Knill's mortal remains as to guide his privateer ships to harbour after plundering the French - and also to aid his smuggling craft, many of them those same privateers as they ghosted home by moonshine.

The procession consists of a fiddler, two elderly widows and ten young daughters of worthy couples Down'long, the vicar, the collector of customs and the mayor, preceded of course by the mace bearers. They all dance - or prance - or shuffle - round the monument, only the little girls making much of a job of it, and chant the Hundredth Psalm. Then the girls,

appropriately white-frocked and all ten or under, sing the Virgins' Song, which was specially composed for the 1801 celebrations and goes thus:

"Shun the bustle of the bay,
Hasten, virgins, come away;
Hasten to the mountain's brow,
Leave, oh leave, St Ives below.
Haste to breathe a purer air,
Virgins fair, and pure as fair;
Fly St Ives and all her treasures,
Fly her soft voluptuous pleasures;
Fly her sons and all the wiles
Lurking in their wanton smiles.
Fly her splendid midnight halls,
Fly the revels of her balls;
Fly, oh fly, the chosen seat,
Where vanity and fashion meet.
Thither hasten, form the ring,
Round the tomb in chorus sing.
And on the loft mountain's brow - aptly dight,
Just as we should be, all in white,
Leave our cowels and our cares below."

"Soft voluptuous pleasures"! "Splendid midnight halls"! They seem to have enjoyed a proper old shindig in the St Ives of 1801 in between trading and tinning and fishing and smuggling! Or do we detect the ghostly tones of Kingston the Reformer who hanged jolly John Payne the portreeve, and Major Ceely the Puritan who smashed up the lovely woodwork of the parish church, still condemning the simple joys of our forebears in Nelson's days?

The song sung, it is the duty of the two widows to report that the ceremonies have been properly observed. Thereupon £25 is distributed from the trust fund as follows: £10 for a dinner at the local hostelry for the mayor, collector and vicar and two friends apiece (a sum which needs supplementing nowadays to an extent the benefactor could never have foreseen!), £15 to be split among fiddler, widows and girls in the procession, and a clerk to record the event - after the purchase of ribbons and an account book. There are other bequests too, equally trivial after many generations of inflation, but in their way priceless. It is but two centuries since John Knill in his immaculate handwriting penned his strange bequest and the conditions thereof. He was a man who craved immortality and is a step along the road to achieving

At Knill's Steeple - the celebrations of 1916.
Sir Edward Hain stands in the centre, surrounded by the girls in white,
while Mayor Tom Uren is on their right. (Photograph courtesy RIC.)

56

it. St Ives is the brighter for his life, smuggling and all.

Up fiddler trails, top-hatted, scraping an air,
Trailing through rhododendrons, gorse and people
Ten white-frocked girls, widows, priest, taxman, mayor:
Quinquennial procession to Knill's Steeple.

Round they jog, hand in hand, little girls shrill
The virgins' song, the funds are shared, all's done;
Stark points the pryamid on Worvas Hill,
Landmark for smuggling and the midnight run.

What was John Knill, in London churchyard laid,
Who built, whose presence fills, the armorial granite?
Collector, mason, mayor. The moonshine trade
Which cheers both Bench and pew -
                                  some say Knill ran it.

Lest fame should fade, this various man's bequest
Grants at his mausoleum to St Ives
A July holiday. Content he'll rest,
Remembrance five more summertimes survives.

It's near two hundred years since first they went,
Maids and all, dancing round Knill's Monument.

A far, far older custom than the Knill's celebrations is
Guise Dancing. It was practised in Penzance and
Scilly besides St Ives, but faded out as other traditions
and customs did with World War Two. Attempts are
made to revive it, but as with hurling, the spirit of the
occasion is dead. Guise dancing had been from time
immemorial a nightly frolic between Christmas Day
and Twelfth Night. There was not much dancing about
it. Bands of mainly young people, men masquerading
as women and women as men, all veiled or black-faced,
came in through the front door - no locked doors in
those fondly remembered times! - to drink a toast,
crack a joke or two while we tried to guess who they
were, and perhaps sing a song we would all join in.
One party of Guise Dancers who used to drop in just
after Christmas for years used to present a rehearsed
programme for good measure (and an adequate
reward!). Up to the eighteen hundreds the Guise
Dancers would perform a St George and the Dragon
play, featuring also a Turkish warrior, Father
Christmas and the King of Egypt's daughter. What an
act! The St George folk-play was a feature of medieval
mumming; and in the mummers, it seems, you will find
the origin of Cornish Guise Dancers, Scillonian Goose
Dancers, and Scottish Guisards. Further back still the
Christmas jollifications are said to have had their
roots in the Roman winter solstice festival - the
Saturnalia - when masters and slaves and mistresses
swopped places and a jolly orgy was enjoyed by all.

Christmas merrymaking was not wholly home-made,
though. Borough Accounts record paying the Robin
Hood Players from St Columb, in North Cornwall,
sixteen shillings and five shillings on two separate
occasions in the 1580s. They performed in the open
air, probably on Twelfth. Night. The accounts also
refer to the erection of stage and props for the mystery
plays - plays about saints and such Bible stories as
Noah and the Flood, performed in Cornish by the local
Guilds or Mysteries - which were a feature of medieval
and later Cornish life. To this day there is a large
following in the town for amateur dramatics and
locally written plays, though these no longer cling to
religious themes! But other customs such as Allan
Apples for children on Allhallows Eve, and the
blowing of May horns at crack of dawn on May Day,
and the Summer Games with their King and Queen and
Maypole, survive not at all, though I was accustomed
to the first two in my girlhood. Gone too are the
Christmas parties with their impromptu concerts
everyone had to do a turn in, and their silly, jolly,
lovely little games.

A hurling match traditionally follows the Feast
Monday ceremonial in early February. In recent years
the Mayor has thrown the ball from the churchyard
wall to youngsters waiting on the beach below. They
scramble for it on the sands, and after a good old romp,
rampage with it to the Guildhall. The ancient game
used to be played with two sides and took place in the
streets, as is done today at St Columb. The ball is like
a cricket ball and is sheathed in silver, got from
hammering a crown or two into a flat foil. The idea of
hurling, which was once popular in all the Celtic
countries, was that two teams, everybody present
joining in, struggled to score a goal in a trough or
basket - this was called "hurling to goal" - or else
surged over the countryside to some designated place
such as a church tower, perhaps three or four miles
away. This was "hurling to country". Both versions

were tough, even dangerous, and on occasion fatal. The historian Carew tells us in 1602 that hurling to goal was a common diversion at Cornish weddings, where guests took on all comers. St Ives used to take on Lelant across country. For a time afterwards the Toms, Wills and Jans opposed everybody else on Porthminster Beach. Now it is a free-for-all for the boys on the harbour sands. It is believed that the hurling of the silver ball into the air in prehistoric times - and you never lose touch with the prehistoric in Penwith - was an act of sympathetic magic to guarantee the growing ascension of the sun in the young year. Feast Monday is, significantly, half-way between winter solstice and spring equinox; and the missionaries who brought us The Word so long ago were adept at tying up pagan with Christian festivals.

For many generations there was keen competition between the St Ives and Lelant hurlers, though eventually the numerical superiority of the St Ives men made the game too one-sided. The boundary between the two bases - the centre line, if you like - was a stone implanted outside Captain Perry's house at Chyangwheal, Carbis Bay, and the goals were the two parish churches. This boundary stone would have been just beyond Trelyon villlage, where the kindred sport of wrestling took place, being on the doorstep, as it were, of its patron Squire Stephens at Tregenna.

Seaward of the village was the upper section of the surface workings of Wheal Margery. This tin mine was being worked in 1770. It ran under the sea between Porthminster Point and Carbis Bay Beach, 121 fathoms - over 700 feet - beneath the sea-bed. Small wonder that the mine was perpetually at odds with seeping sea-water! Wheal Margery 'Count House stood at the corner of Love Lane, the top road leading to Tregenna Castle and once the main road past the Cornish Arms into St Ives. 'Count House was demolished when the present A30 came into being; but Mr Couch's forge behind the pub was still exuding burning hoof smell and steam and resounding with the merry clank of hammer on anvil when I was a youngster.

Today a stately mansion stands among trees where mine workings sprawled muddy and busy and the main shaft descended so deep. This is Treloyhan Manor, built and its surroundings landscaped in 1890 for Sir

Edward Hain, Shipowner of St Ives.

For sixty years the Hain Steamship Company operated one of the world's best and oldest tramp steamer fleets. Its big freighters did not run on regular routes, but picked up a cargo here, discharged it there, loaded anew for yet another port across wide oceans. Company offices were at St Ives, opposite the library at the foot of Tregenna Hill, where a few scratchy pen nibs would seal the romance of the seven seas in a ledger, like a genie in a bottle. The offices were later shifted to Cardiff and then to London, but not in Sir Edward's lifetime. He, founder of the Steamship Company, gazes down from his portrait in the Hain Collection at St Ives Museum. He resembles King George V. But he was not the first Edward Hain, ship-owner. In 1802 Edward Hain, Master Mariner of St Ives, married Mary Williams. Their son, Edward Hain II, was in 1837 Master and Owner of the schooner *Camilla,* alternatively rigged as a brigantine and dashingly painted so in the museum. In due course he owned a fleet of sailing vessels, taking several to sea himself. He gave *Camilla* to his son Edward Hain III when his future successor was twenty-three. These Hain ships were sturdy craft. They sailed mainly in European and Mediterranean waters, though the *Margaret Hain* traded as far afield as Rio and New York. She was a brigantine, built at Rye in 1866 of oak and finished off in teak, 108 feet 6 inches long, 24 feet in beam and 13 feet from deck through to keel.

Edward Hain III, ambitious and like his father often at sea in command, was "frightened", we are told, by his son's plans for steamships. His fears did not prevent young Edward Hain IV from visiting Redhead's yards at South Shields in May 1878, and signing a contract for an 1800-ton iron steamer SS *Trewidden* at £1 a ton. From then on Rehead's built 84 Hain steamships, the earliest of them being rigged for sail too.

SS *Trewidden* made quite a stir in St Ives, as you can imagine. Mr W. J. Jacobs recounts how "she was launched on the eve of a shipping boom, and for the first year the shareholders received 20%. The shares were divided into sixty-fourths. My grandfather, Mr William Johns, took one sixty-fourth. The Bolitho family of Penzance (they were bankers) gave their substantial backing to the scheme and Messrs Edward

Two views of Porthminster Beach in the 1920s as seen (above) from
Porthminster Point and (below) from Pedn Olva. Both show seine boats
drawn up on the beach below the station. Photographs by F. H. Green.

Hain & Son by using the name of Bolitho were able to obtain several shareholders in West Cornwall, but after they had approached all potential subscribers there were six shares unsubscribed. The promoters approached the original shareholders again, my grandfather was one one of those who agreed to take a second share, and eventually the *Trewidden* shareholding was complete.

"After such a promising start Messrs Edward Hain & Son had little difficulty in floating another steamship named *Tregenna*. Other vessels followed in rapid succession so that by the time the 1914 war broke out the Hain Steamship Company was the largest tramp shipping concern in the country. During its existence scores of St Ives men manned these ships as captains, officers, engineers and seamen, and the company's name gave St Ives a prominent place in the shipping world."

Sir Edward founded the Hain Steamship Company in 1901, in £10 shares and with half a million capital. It brought a lot of money into the town, and for Edward Hain IV riches and a knighthood. He built his splendid mansion above St Ives. A distinguished family had become great and must, it seemed, become greater. But it was not to be. His only son, the fifth Edward, was killed at Gallipoli in 1915 and Sir Edward himself died two years later. In that year, 1917, P & O bought up Hain's at £80 a share - a bonanza to local investors! - but the Company retained its title and management. The takeover was completed in a ship at anchor in St Ives Bay by Lord Inchcape and Mr Robert Read of St Ives, Chairman of Hain's.

Not so long ago the Company finally lost its identity in the greater unit of P & O, but we look back with pride on a century and a half of commerce, seamanship, war and grim adventure. In the first World War, 18 Tre-boats were lost by enemy action, in the second 28, with over 40,000 officers and men; 28 out of 32 ships with the "H" symbol on their funnels! One, SS *Trevanion*, was sunk by the German pocket battleship *Graf Spee*, having first contrived to radio her position and so bring her avengers on the scene and the *Spee* to destruction off Montevideo. The *Trevanion*'s crew finished up in the Nazi hell-ship *Altmark*, and were rescued in a Norwegian fjord by HMS *Cossack*. But the most famous episode in the history of Hain's was when three-quarters of the *Trevessa*'s crew, their ship having foundered in a hurricane in the Indian Ocean, reached land after sailing over 1500 miles in open boats.

Treloyhan Manor, built for the fifth and future Edward Hains, shipowners, who sadly were not to be, is now a Methodist holiday home. Consuming most of Wheal Margery, it provides an imposing, leafy approach to the town, a drop curtain as it were for the view which bursts upon you as you reach the coastguard houses. But much of old Trelyon village remains. One dwelling that has vanished, though, was Trelyon farmhouse in Steeple Lane, where some relations of mine lived. I was told that in several of the cottages there you could hear at night the miners at work in the shallow galleries of Wheal Venture, on the borders of Carbis Bay and the haunts of my happy childhood.

Another of F. H. Green's evocative studies of St Ives in the '20s.

Part of the area that came to be known as Carbis Bay - a map by W. Willis dating from the middle of the 19th century. The main St Ives - Lelant road is clearly marked, running from top to bottom. Notice the large number of mine shafts marked in the area of Higher Carbence and north of Carninney. These belonged to Wheal Providence.

CHAPTER V

CARBIS BAY AS KNOWN AND TOLD

Carbis Bay was the beginning and the end of everything for me when I was a child. So much to do; so much to see; but now how changed! The beach was a fair distance from my home up there on the road, and not to be visited save with mother or one of my several aunts. But abandoned mines, "knacked" - as they used to say - up to forty years before, were nearer home. They were a playground for a little girl often alone, yet, with a wealth of interest to claim her imagination, never bored or lonely. Besides, there were always friendly cats around, there were surface workings and derelict mine buildings to explore, and joy of joy! a bank of wild strawberries.

The mine dump behind Great Aunt Margaret's Sycamore House rose red and enormous, a landmark for a century and a half that some years ago was bulldozed over the adjoining acres in the course of so-called development. To climb this was an adventure, with its scree of rubble, and the turf on the summit which was the only living thing that could grow there, and the wary seagulls that took off with screams of alarm as you scrambled to the top.

In the shallow mine ponds were frogs to reach for and tadpoles to catch. We local children were brought up to be aware of the dangers of the "bal", though. I would never venture closer to the yawning shafts than to toss a stone over the encircling drystone wall, and count as it bounded hollowly from side to side until with an echoing plop it hit water deep, deep down.

Up towards Knill's Steeple were the furzey downs, a playground further afield but today for the most part forgotten beneath roof tops. The bracken there, brown and scratchy in winter, in spring grew head-high to me; an impenetrable jungle. Clearings and lanes became bright with primroses and bluebells, cowslips and campions and wild flowers of every kind and colour inviting me to pick them, all set like gems in the prevailing gold of the gorse. While May and June transformed the whole area round the Steeple into a lilac wonderland of rhododendrons in bloom. Happy days!

Above all there were the Great Aunts to visit. Mary Anne and Elizabeth reared my mother, one of the ten children of their brother Francis, and I loved them as she did. It was good to have been brought up in such love. While for their house Idris I have much love too, however it has altered over the years. Great Aunt Margaret, "Pretty She" as she was known in the family, existed so far as I was concerned to be aggravated. I took delight in it, as a small child would. To the other great aunts I was indifferent - or I was kept away from them, I don't know which. They all carried walking sticks. In later years I concluded that this was solely to touch me up and keep me in order. None of my great uncles survived to greet, in whatever way they deemed appropriate, their great niece. The aunts - they were all on my mother's side of the family - lived at Chyangwheal or Carbis Water.

Carbis Bay straddles a mile or so of the main road, and has engulfed three or four hamlets which were still separate at the turn of the century. The village got its collective name only when the Great Western Railway opened its St Erth - St Ives branch line in 1877. The new viaduct, like all the viaducts in West Cornwall a handsome structure, crossed Carbis Valley, which was once busy with tin mining but is now quiet and green with trees. It almost crossed the top of the beach, too, the passengers in the train enjoying that magnificent view of St Ives Bay which still takes my breath away. So the GWR called their pretty station - and how pretty it used to be! - Carbis Bay, picking the words out in masses of flowers on the bank facing the platform. The name spread to the whole district. Carbis Water had been known as Carbus in 1659, Carbousse or Carbeasse in 1617, Carbisse in 1585 and Carbous in 1391. That is the origin of Carbis; a time-honoured name meaning in Old Cornish either "cart bridge" or "the road to the

Lelant Station, on the St Ives Branch. The photograph shows Brunel's broad gauge line, and was probably taken in the 1880s. (Courtesy RIC)

earthworks".

Coming up from St Ives past Treloyhan Manor and the Cornish Arms you arrive at Chyangwheal, "the house by the field" and mentioned in 1649. The next hamlets were Higher Carbence and Lower Carbence, from which Carbis Water led down to Carbis Valley. Further towards Lelant Boskerris Lane led inland to Boskerris Wartha and Boskerris Woolas ("higher place" and "lower place"), two farm hamlets now submerged in modern buildings. The highroad led out of Carbis Bay across Longstone Downs, the long-stone being a pagan monolith the cattle in the fields used to scratch themselves against. Part way down the hill you will still find Wink Town, of which there is a tale to tell later on.

That is how Carbis Bay must have been before the railway came and ribbon development took over. Its boundary with St Ives would have run just above the pub, perhaps along Wheal Venture Road on the one side, and on the other down Lang's Lane past Little Park Owles to the Hain Walk and the foreshore. Opposite the farmhouse and its adjoining cottages at Chyangwheal stood the village pump, out of use before my time though tap water was still far from universal in the district. George Kemp farmed Chyangwheal Farm. He had married Katie Perry, who with her sister Mary had inherited it from their father Andrew Perry.

George Kemp had spent many of his early years in South Africa, which, because cheap alluvial tin from Malaya had driven the expensively produced Cornish tin out of the market, and "the bals had been knacked", was the Mecca of Cornishmen in the later 1800s. When an old man he told me of a never-to-be-forgotten adventure there, which is recorded in history as the last instance of a British private army. Working their way north from Capetown, George Kemp and his partner got to Johannesburg with nothing more than a voracious appetite and the clothes they stood up in. There they heard of prospects better to their liking than slaving underground with fellow "Cousin Jacks". Someone in the town was offering good pay, a horse and a rifle to whomsoever would serve under a Dr Jameson who was a friend of the great Cecil Rhodes.

In due course they rode with six hundred other half-trained recruits into the Transvaal - and slap into an ambush. Rows of marksmen appeared along the ridges of the hills, cannon were swung into position, and Jameson was summoned to surrender. There was nothing for it but to do so. And what of Farmer George and his six hundred comrades? They were all rounded up and disarmed, guarded a day or two in a compound, and then shipped off to England - with a permanent ban on re-entry. The Jameson Raid triggered off the Boer War.

Beside the farm at Chyangwheal runs an access to Fuggoe Lane, where more cottages stood on the site of an Iron Age settlement, complete with an underground, tunnel-like structure skilfully built of arching, interlocking drystone, curving slightly and with lintelled doorways. You can see one like it at Chapel Euny, Sancreed - a fogou, an integral part of the prehistoric villages of the far South West. Further references to Carbis Bay's fogou appear in such documents as the Uny Lelant Rent Charge Book of 1839; "Fuggoe Croft" and "Croft Little Fuggoe". Opinion is undecided on whether fogous were primarily storage depots or part of the village defences when under attack. There would have been several reasons for building such an elaborate structure and doubtless every purpose was served. Mr Morton Nance, Grand Bard of Cornwall, who lived at Carbis Bay, discovered a flint manufactory on the site, proving the existence of the ancient village if not the precise use of its fogou. Nothing is to be seen here today but modern houses and the lane, which is intact. But I fear the "march of progress" will jack-boot that out of sight, too, before the century is through.

Seaward of Chyangwheal, Pannier Lane curved steeply down to the mines, which overlooked the beach. Richard Pearce, who married Great Aunt Margaret and was born in 1840, described to my father how files of mules and donkeys used to be driven up it laden with ore, a pannier or basket slung on each flank, or in sacks across the animal's back. It was a common sight in his younger days. He also recalled a "wink" on the main road above, and a cluster of cottages down the lane. None of them survived to my time, when nothing but fields lay between Chyangwheal and the sea, not even Valley Road.

The present Counthouse Lane did then lead inland to Wheals Speed and Providence, turning off the highway beside Idris, where Aunts Mary Anne and Elizabeth lived and of which I cherish such precious memories. Idris was built in the 1700s and generations of my family lived there. Until 1900 it was called Bay View. Bay Views and Sea Views abounded in Carbis Bay once sea views became fashionable, and profitable. There has been a further change of name since the 1939 war - to Count House Cottage. Great Aunt Mary Anne was born at Idris in 1834 and died there ninety years afterwards.

Idris's front garden leads down to the main road. I used to sit on the hedge watching the neighbours and the horses and carts and carriages and bicycles go by, the cattle being herded to St Ives from Helston market, the occasional motor car, and once a year the circus parading for its local booking. This was the highlight of life at Carbis Bay. I had to be up on that hedge at six in the morning to see the horses and elephants and caravans troop past. The caravans were all of course the old-fashioned gipsy sort that are so much more romantic than today's. The procession would turn left into Chyangwheal farmyard and thence into the field at the rear. There the Big Top was erected with a speed and proficiency that amazed those villagers who could get off work, chores or school to behold the transformation scene.

The Circus gave a matinee and an evening performance, and no-one would have missed the show for worlds. Droves of St Ives folk plodded up the hill in couples and in families to revel in this spectacular interlude in what was, I suppose, a pretty humdrum existence, when even the public tooth-drawing my father told me of was an event to laugh about for weeks afterwards. I can see in my mind's eye the clowns, the bare-back riders, the high-wire acrobats and every other act on the programme. I can also see the Kemps and Miss Perry lording it in the best seats at the ring side, in courtesy of their generous loan of the field. How I envied them! By next morning the whole circus was packed up and on its way to another site, but I liked to think of it as existing just for us; an event which occurred like Christmas and birthdays to bring glitter and excitement and enjoyment to our quiet community.

From the approach to the counthouse (converted to today's handsome dwelling) and the two mines the main road continued past Rose and Myrtle cottages and three very pretty cottages side-on to the highway. They huddled together, with long steps leading up to each. They are still occupied - all but one which was demolished for road widening. Mrs Cowling's shop was opposite, with Wayside Cottage attached. All these cottages lay in the shadow of the mine dump - the towering red slag-heap already mentioned.

Round the bend and down the short hill to the shop now, but not then, on the corner! Road levelling had necessitated a great granite retaining wall, on top of which Wheal Providence workings stretched up and away into the country. Close to the wall was a mineshaft with a ladder reaching to surface. I have seen it, but never dared descent - not only for fear of family reprisals. However, men did use the shaft long after the mine was closed. It provided a short cut to Carbis Valley and the station and was, you might say, the first pedestrian subway ever! It caved in beside the railway track in 1990. The station, by the way, was built on East Providence ropewalk.

Fernhill was a large house beside Carbis Valley. It was built in the mid-1800s by a Mr Edwin Kelly. He fell in love with the valley; the house, down a long, wooded drive which hides it from the road, was the result. A house further down the valley, Glenside, was a second offspring of this devoted attachment. It was known as the "dower house" and one of his sisters, Mrs Jenkyn, I am told lived there. His other sister, Mrs Sampson, resided at Fernhill.

Fernhill was the home of Dr Rice when I was young. He was esteemed as a brilliant physician. He drove a brown, open car at a time when Carbis Bay traffic was almost exclusively horse-drawn. There were horse buses, Jersey cars and wagonettes, carriages, traps and jingles, carts and drays and hay-wains, and humble donkey-shays; few riding horses, though - they'd been commandeered for the cavalry at the front, and by the time the survivors got home motor-bikes and cars were taking over. Dr Rice's motor car was a novelty for quite a while. He was conspicuously tall, with bright red hair; and a back injury making him walk unusually erect, both driving and afoot he always attracted

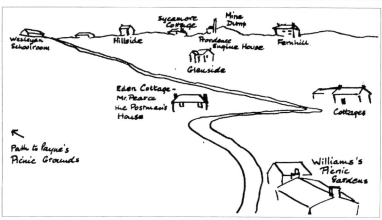

Wesleyan Schoolroom

Hillside

Sycamore Cottage

Mine Dump

Providence Engine House

Fernhill

Glenside

Eden Cottage - Mr. Pearce the Postman's House

Cottages

Path to Payne's Picnic Grounds

Williams's Picnic Gardens

The Carbis Valley, looking inland
towards Wheal Providence.
The photograph, dating from about 1900,
is from the RIC's collection.

respectful attention. He had a dear little wife and one daughter, Helen, who danced beautifully and did the choreography for Mary Reed's productions - amateur of course and entirely local - at the wooden Institute now replaced by the Memorial Hall.

Fernhill was a most attractive house with a breathtaking view of St Ives Bay. It was approached through a large white gate at the lower end of the drive. By this gate was a smaller one. It opened on to a narrow path which led down through the woods to the bottom of the valley by Glenside, and was a right-of-way which, like many other cherished footpaths, seems to have been obliterated. Right up to World War Two people, at any rate in West Cornwall, used to collect their medicine from the surgery, commonly at the doctor's house. It was dispensed on the premises. As a child I would volunteer at any time to fetch someone's medicine; not, I regret, from an urge for community service, but because in Dr Rice's conservatory, through which you reached his front door, two parrots swung in cages. They swore fluently and without prompting, "just like poetry", and no-one admired them more than I.

The next place to mention at Carbence is Sycamore Cottage, just past Fernhill drive. Here was the first sub-Post Office, I believe, in Carbis Bay. Across the road was Sycamore House. Its drive was as long as Fernhill's and was overhung by the avenue of splendid sycamores which gave the place its name. Much of the drive was lost when the road width was doubled, while the house as I knew it has disappeared behind an imposing façade which in no way resembles that of the 'twenties. It used to be a charming house, built in the granite blocks of its period to last for ever. Double green gates were at the foot of the drive, and the garden was a joy to behold.

Great Aunt Margaret lived here with her husband Uncle Richard Pearce, whose pride and joy the garden was. He and I were not fond of each other, I suppose because I would pick his flowers while he was determined that I should not. He could not run as fast as I could; he had a wooden leg, following a mining accident in Colorado. The Pearces owned a carriage drawn by a black horse called Tom. If I was very good they would take me to St Ives with them. I sat on the front seat with my back to the horse and facing Aunt Margaret. In St Ives we always put up at Jimmy Nicholls's hostelry at the bottom of Tregenna Hill. Jimmy's yard was enclosed by the old Poor House. When the big Workhouse "over the hill" at Madron was built, the helpless inmates were moved thither from their home environment, their former quarters eventually becoming the Borough Surveyor's store.

A cottage or two lay between Uncle Richard's green gates and Carbis Water, the stream which rose near Knill's Steeple. One particularly pretty cottage, since demolished to make way for the shop at the corner, stood side-on to the main road. It had faced the little river and the tiny wooden bridge which crossed it there longer than could be remembered, and led up ancient steps to Wheal Providence mine. Back across the road were more cottages. You had to go down steps to get to them. The one next door to Sycamore Cottage, beautifully done up now and enjoying a magnificent view over the Bay, was once the home of Mrs Frazier, an elderly lady who kept a shop there, in competition with Mrs Cowling's immaculate general stores adjoining Wayside higher up the hill. Mrs Frazier was a nice old soul and her shop was heaven for children. Nothing was tidy. Lard and butter, unpackaged then and weighed before the customer's eyes, were kept alongside the paraffin, bootlaces, ham, dusters, dried fish ("tow-rag" in the vernacular), soap, lemonade powder and whatever else comes to mind. There were stone ginger beer bottles and lemonade bottles with marbles in the neck to be pushed down in a gust of fizz before you could pour out or drink. The shop had no counter, only shelves. Sweets were everywhere. Sticks of barley sugar peeped from jars, liquorice laces trailed from boxes, boxes of sweets were placed wherever space could be found or were dumped on the floor, and liquorice "All sorts" were piled in profusion. Sweets have never since tasted so good as those I bought from Mrs Frazier. Mrs Frazier's cottage - the shop was a lean-to - has been beautifully renovated by a well-known artist and is now called "Clair de Lune". In the next house but one in Carbis Valley lived a neat and lively little woman, Mrs Benjamin Rowe. Her husband, who had built the house, very properly named it "Hillside". Recently, though, it has acquired a new name - "Bobtails"! I wonder, is this progress? And what would Mrs

Benjamin Rowe have made of it? Knowing her, I think she would have taken to her bed!

Carbis Valley was bustling with mining activity during the last century, mine workings extending to the beach. Carbis Water was used for tin-streaming the whole way down the valley, independent tinners washing from the tailings of the mines above tin that it had not been worth the Company's while to extract. In 1646 and '47 there was a vastly different use for the stream. When the plague visited St Ives all contact with the borough and its environs was suspended. Quarantine was rigorously enforced, the boundaries being fixed at Polmantor, west of the stricken town, and at Carbis Water. There where the highway crossed the stream (today it is piped beneath the road) the townsfolk placed their money in the water at the ford, as told before.

On the Lelant side of Carbis Water, Carbis Bay's first Wesleyan Chapel was built. Opposite was a footpath leading to the railway station. There was no Boskerris Road then, just fields and another village pump.

I never knew Carbis Bay other than as the ribbon development which followed the railway. But there were gaps in it, wide gaps, mostly to the north'ard and all filled in now. Field after field stretched down to the sea. You gazed across grass to blue water, the wide fringe of the tide out of sight under the cliff, St Ives to the west and Godrevy east within the wide arc of the horizon making the loveliest view in the land. But when the northerly gales blew and a few giant waves filled the bay, you could hardly look to sea for the rain and spray and spindrift that the wind whipped up the slope. Past the chapel a rough track led inland to the two Boskerris farms. On the other side you came to Sea View Cottage which with much added to it is now Lindsay Court. Then there were the crossroads, where Longstone farm stood. Its granite cowsheds are delightful houses today. Trencrom Road boasted a few cottages, while there were more down on Longstone Hill.

On Longstone Downs there was a battle, or at any rate a skirmish, during the Civil War. Cornwall was almost wholly for the King; St Ives, ever remarkable for an independent approach to affairs, was for Parliament and the Commonwealth. The food levy imposed on the town for provisioning King Charles's Cornish army was a grievous burden. When in 1645, the royalist cause being in decline, St Ives judged the time ripe for revolt, Sir Richard Grenville force-marched down through the county and scattered the rebel recruits assembled on Longstone Downs, as has been told in the first chapter. Dire retribution followed with the mayor imprisoned and fined and a couple of citizens dragged off for execution.

Longstone was the venue for an encounter of another kind in July 1820; a sporting fixture. It was a wrestling match between St Ives and St Just, a two-day event supported by the local gentry and almost everybody else thereabouts, with even wilder enthusiasm and placing of bets than at the cockfighting up at the Heath Cottage amphitheatre near the Steeple. It began on the 24th and finished at dusk on the 25th. St Just won.

Between Longstone crossroads and Boskerris Lane an apparition was seen that was last reported around 1850. I doubt if you will see it again. A lady hurrying home from Lelant in the starlight saw a tall-hatted figure standing on the hedge to her right. About to exchange those passing greetings with which one saluted acquaintance and stranger alike in Cornwall she halted, the "Good evening" freezing on her lips. The figure had no face! She ran all the way home and fainted. On hearing the tale her friends laughed at her, but an old local preacher - and what more solid evidence could you get? - said he had seen it too.

At Wink Town (the "town" here being no more than a cluster of cottages) there was an ale house, a humble pub with a limited licence that restricted its sales to beer and such and excluded spirits. This pub was known to enlightened customers as a "wink" or to give it its full name, a "kiddleywink". Wherever you went in Cornwall the "kiddle" was the promise of hospitality. Perpetually topped up and steaming either on the hob or swinging from its hook over the peat and furze fire, it was common alike to kitchen and tap-room. In inns such as that at Wink Town a wink and a nod towards the kiddle, or kettle, would if you were known or vouched for conjure up as much brandy, geneva or rum as you'd a taste for; even tea if that's what you

The first Carbis Bay Mayor of Greater St Ives, Ald. W. P. Toy,
photographed outside the St Uny Hotel.

preferred - it was far dearer in the shops. It was all brought across the Channel, duty free from France, by those criminals of the coast - or were they heroes? - the smugglers.

A little below Wink Town are crossroads, where in years gone by one dared not venture after dark. At any moment during the night a phantom coach might come rumbling from that tunnel of elms at Laity Lane, out across the main road, and into Church Lane. It would vanish there, a spectral interlude one was thankful to have experienced by hearsay only, particularly since the driver was a female ghost.

The association of phantom coaches with kiddleywinks is a Cornish phenomenon. When a "run" was under way it was necessary to keep people indoors. The less folk knew of what was afoot, the less chance the Revenue Officers had of interfering. It was essential, too, to provide a reason, plausible 150 years ago, for hoof-beats and the crunch and creak of cart wheels at an hour when honest men were abed. As for the ghost on the hedge - a look-out, would you say? with scarf drawn up to his eyes, and the shadow of his hat, and starlight. As faceless as your modern villain in his nylon stocking headgear!

Kipling sums it all up:

> "Five and twenty ponies
> Trotting through the dark -
> Brandy for the Parson,
> 'Baccy for the Clerk;
> Laces for a lady, letters for a spy,
> Watch the wall, my darling,
> while the gentlemen go by!"

THE LONGSTONE COACH

The night blows wild on Longstone Downs,
A pewter moon through the cloud-wrack frowns,
And Winktown cottagers abed
Under the blankets hide their head.

"Hark, rain rattling upon the pane!
How the trees creak up Trencrom Lane!"
"'Tes the rattle of wheels at the crossroads here,
The creak of the ghastly coach, my dear."

"Hush! Hold me, lover, like we'm asleep;
It's the Coach for sure, and death to peep!
The tramp of its headless horses drowns
Even the wind on Longstone Downs."

So, curtains drawn and none to spy,
Horse and cart go rumbling by
With kegs for kiddleywink, vestry, Hall
And a fig for Customs, my handsomes all!

Great Aunt Elizabeth, about 17 years old. The photograph is dated c.1865.

CHAPTER VI

AUNTS, CHAPELS AND PICNICS

Idris at Chyangwheal was, as I have indicated, dear to me. It was my second home. I used to lie in bed watching the beams of Godrevy lighthouse revolving. Their rays would sweep across the ceiling of my bedroom overlooking the Bay. Virginia Woolf, the famous authoress who lived at Talland House, St Ives, would also watch it flashing; it inspired her to write her novel *To the Lighthouse*. There was no such inspiration for the little girl at Idris. But I do remember it as a real comfort which could send me to sleep like a lullaby, whilst last glimpses as I drifted off would be of the red flashes of Trevose Head away on the horizon. Godrevy Light, alas! revolves no longer. It just switches on and off. Now Trinity House question its future.

The lighthouse was built in 1859 to warn shipping off the dangerous reef known as The Stones, which extends a mile or so across St Ives Bay. You can watch the waves breaking over the reef, or a slow swell heaving over it, while at low tide its peaks jag above the restless surface. Three keepers manned the lighthouse, and there have been times when storms prevented their relief week after week. But even in the worst weather, when of course it was needed most, the sentinel of the reef, perched on its islet and rather resembling a ship itself, never failed to warn passing vessels. It was manned until 1934, when it became automatic, and that somehow assuring revolving of the beam was reduced to a soul-less blip. One night in 1975, for the first time in 116 years, there was no light in the lighthouse. It had gone electric, and a windmill the authorities were experimenting with to generate current for the lantern had broken down. So much for modern times!

My great aunts' kitchen was a large one, unaltered, I had been told, over a hundred years. In it were two long tables, uncovered as kitchen tables then were. One was of deal and the other of red pine, their tops smooth and soft from daily scrubbing. There was a dresser full of beautiful china, and beside it a grandfather clock relentlessly ticking the hours away. In the corner a "what-not" groaned with more china, while on the mantlepiece the usual spotted china cows lined up with brass candlesticks and the three-legged bell-metal saucepan or skillet, each item in its appointed place and not to be touched except for cleaning. I have all these knick-knacks now, and value them greatly.

At the end of one of the long tables a large copper pan covered with a cloth was always kept full of saffron cake - made of real saffron and quite different from today's substitute. This was for any caller to enjoy with a "dish o' tay". Visitors had often walked a long way, and were ready for such prompt refreshment as pan and kettle ever boiling on the hob provided. The hob was a Cornish range, gleaming with brasswork, that had been set into an open fireplace and was, in its day, the last word in kitchen equipment. Not all the callers had set out to visit Aunt Mary Anne and Aunt Lizzie. It was just that the long trudge uphill from St Ives, with the prospect of as far still to go before getting home, often proved too much for ageing feet. In my young days there was no St Ives - Carbis Bay bus service, just the GWR branch line; and it was such a distance to and from the station if you lived away on the downs that you might as well walk.

My aunts' kitchen led up by four wooden steps into the back kitchen. Its open hearth had a large iron door closed across it and I never saw it used. In the middle of the floor was the pump, which stood over a well. No water was laid on to Carbis Bay until the turn of the century. Even then the new houses still had to pump the mains water up to the cistern in the roof. Hard work it was, too! The aunts' venture into the twentieth century so far was to have a tap put over the sink.

There was no sewerage at Carbis Bay when I was a child, no electricity, nor gas, nor street lighting. The

St Ives lamplighter used to tramp up the hill turning the gas lamps on with his long pole, but his tour of duty ended where the pavement ended, opposite the Cornish Arms. Thence the "parish lantern" up there in the sky alone lit up the night. The first street lighting at Carbis Bay was installed in the early thirties, when a calor gas lamp was fitted to the outer wall of the chemist's shop at Carbis Water. Soon Carbis Bay was to have the benefit of a full electricity service.

When electricity was first brought to the houses here, around 1920, it cost £5 a point to instal. Hitherto we had relied on oil lamps, candles and candle-lit lanterns for night excursions. Carriage lamps had a thin brass cylinder projecting from the base, a spring pushing the candle up as it burned. It was the great age of paraffin and paraffin wax. However, the headlamps of the few cars of my childhood used acetylene gas, produced by a device which dropped water on to chunks of carbide. It was quite a good light with a peculiar smell, and was also favoured by such cyclists as were able to dip into their pockets to replace the old paraffin bicycle lamp.

But back to Idris, typical of many homes in West Cornwall at that time, though probably better off than most in that several members of the family were sending home considerable sums from abroad.

Besides the kitchen there were two parlours, and a dining room crammed with old books and yet more china. Upstairs were four double bedrooms, the largest Aunt Mary Anne's. She slept in a four-poster bed. If I wanted to see her before she came downstairs, and I often did, I had to knock on the door and then go in. I would find her sitting in the window, reading the enormous Bible on a table there and plaiting her pigtails, ultimately to be wound round her head. She was very old by now, already approaching her nineties, though still tall and upright. She kept her walking stick by her bed, so I knew I had to be good. Then I would fetch a stool and sit at her side. She would recite to me, and tell me stories of fairies and the piskies and spriggans. Goodness knows how often she had had to turn her apron, when piskey-led while walking over Worvas Downs after dark. Once the apron was turned all would be as vivid as in daylight, and she knew exactly where she was.

Turning your clothes always frightened off the little people. One night a neighbour at Chyangwheal found the spriggans counting their gold in her bedroom. They left her a coin when they went away, and were frequent visitors. At last while they were counting she turned her shift and away they fled, leaving their treasure behind. She bought a house at St Ives with it, and lived there a wealthy woman to the end of her days. But when she put her shift on, it gave her such a terrible sensation that she never dared wear it again.

In Aunt Mary Anne's mahogany chest of drawers she kept a gold velvet tea cosy. In it she stored golden sovereigns and half-sovereigns. On my birthday and at Christmas she would ceremoniously produce the tea cosy and present me with a sovereign or a half-sovereign. I still have the gold velvet tea cosy, which has never been used for tea, and I sometimes think that I have only to put my hand in it to find a sovereign there. Perhaps one day the fairies and piskeys will oblige!

I had never seen snow, but had heard about it. Grown-ups still talked about the Great Blizzard of 1891, when there were nine-foot drifts between Carbis Bay and Lelant; there has been nothing like it since. And the snow had lasted. Even during the hay-harvesting in West Cornwall at midsummer that year snow still lay on the ground. When I asked my aunt what made the snow, she told me that it was the old woman in the sky shaking the feathers out of her tie. Ties were mattresses stuffed with feathers, and needed constant shaking. They lay on wooden slats, at any rate on the old-fashioned bedsteads like those at Idris, springs not having been introduced nor spring mattresses even invented.

SNOW IN CORNWALL

That old woman in the sky
    Spent last night, the wise ones say,
Shaking, shaking her feather tie:
    We'll never get to town today.

Hedge to hedge, the turnpike road
    Winds milestone deep, no verge revealed;
Trees are silver lace; it's snowed
    So thick you can't tell lane from field.

Noses press against the pane;
    No one's about; but who's afraid
If, as mum says, it snows again?
    A snowman's waiting to be made.

Slim slots of fox and fitcher show,
    Bird starvelings print an arrowed track:
A sliding eiderdown of snow
    Leaves cottage ridge and chimney black.

Snow laps the launders; windows blink
    When icy loops sag low and break.
Bleak New Year! But the children think
    Cornwall has turned to Christmas cake.
                                        (1979)
    (Fitcher: vixen.   Launder: gutter.)

Until the late years of the nineteenth century, when they were quite old, my aunts used to walk to Penzance to bank their money. There were no banks nearer than that. They would walk over Worvas Downs to Nancledra, then past Kenegie and into Penzance. And back of course, swinging their lanterns as they hurried home at nightfall, fearing no-one in those civilised days but dead scared of the piskeys.

Lizzie was the youngest of the three great aunts. She did not in the least resemble her sisters, being short and pretty, with her black hair hanging in ringlets. Their mother took her and Margaret to Guernsey for their education. We had relations there, like many other Cornish families. Close ties existed between Cornwall and the Channel Islands, particularly throughout the smuggling years which were now past their heyday. At one time Cornish ships had been transferred from home ports to Guernsey, where they were free from the attentions of the Preventive officers, and presumably some of the families of management and crew went there too. I have never heard that my forebears had participated in these nefarious activities, though I do not doubt that some at least of them enjoyed the fruits thereof. What did come from Guernsey were the presents my great-grandmother, who was born in 1803, brought home for the children who had been left behind during her various visits. I have some of them to this day.

Great Aunt Elizabeth was very musical and had a rich, powerful singing voice, both of which talents she dedicated to the chapels which were her life. In the small Chyangwheal New Connexion Chapel, which was built in 1856, she played the harmonium as a labour of love for twenty-five years without missing a single service. The building became the Sunday School on the completion of a larger chapel adjoining it. Aunt Lizzie laid a stone for this chapel in 1901, and with her sister gave the organ chamber to house the splendid new organ there. This gift was in memory of their favourite brother Henry, who died aged 58 in 1894.

Aunt Lizzie's voice dominated the hymns. The preacher might announce that verse so-and-so was to be omitted, but no hymn was going to get past Aunt Lizzie without running its full course. Straight through she would go, with me blushing and embarrassed beside her and her successor at the ivories getting the message by way of the ringing rafters, and the congregation had to follow. Ministers who knew her took the easy line and omitted nothing.

The story of Great Aunt Lizzie's courtship still amuses the family. She was engaged, pretty little miss that she was, to an eligible young man who went to America to make his fortune. This took him thirty years, after which he returned in triumph to claim his bride. Courting was well under way when he remarked that he had once taken his landlady's daughter to the opera.

"Then you may go back to America and continue taking the landlady's daughter to the opera," declares Aunt Lizzie, slamming the matrimonial door for ever. A very Victorian situation, don't you think?

Great Uncle Henry was known in the family as "Captain R". Why the "R" I never knew. He came home from the "States" to retire, and being a bachelor lived with his sisters. A mining engineer, he had been a pioneer of the great Calumet & Hecla copper mine on Lake Superior. His absorbing hobby was astronomy. This he shared with Rev. Balmer Jones, his companion of many a starry night and studious hour. I have his big telescope and his books on the moon and stars. Canon Balmer Jones was Vicar of St Ives. My paternal grandfather, you will recall, built the Mariners' Church to his memory Down'long. Uncle

Henry got the organ loft at Chyangwheal to his, while a stained glass window in the chapel is dedicated to another brother of Elizabeth and Mary Anne, Great Uncle William. He never went overseas but was captain of mines at Redruth. "Captain" was the title the Cornish always accorded their mine managers.

Ardent Methodists though they were, it was to the church that my great uncles and aunts were brought for baptism and burial. All of them were christened at St Ives parish church - Mary Anne the eldest in 1834, Henry in 1836, and then Margaret and Thomas and my grandfather Francis. Finally Uncle William and Aunt Elizabeth stood together at the font in 1856, aged ten and eight respectively. The first christening occurred before the earliest Carbis Bay chapel was consecrated, so it was to the church with you or nowhere. But why my old people, who rest generation by generation in Lelant churchyard, were not baptised there too I cannot say.

Carbis Bay life then revolved around the Methodist New Connexion chapel at Chyangwheal and the Wesleyan Chapel at Boskerris. Where Chyangwheal New Connexion Chapel stands today, with its new roof and large and generous membership, 150 years ago Carbis Bay Methodists and Wesleyans were holding joint open-air services. On the two congregations parting company - a parting that was to stay - the Wesleyans built their little chapel at Carbis Water in 1835. A larger one was opened on almost the same site fifty years later and the earlier chapel demolished. It became a Sunday School - now Thurlstone House - when the Boskerris chapel was opened in 1903. This has a fine stained glass window, subscribed for by Dolcoath miners as a memorial to their late managing director Captain Josiah Thomas.

The Thomases were Wesleyans of Camborne. Captain Josiah had contracted the miners' dread lung disease and moved to Carbis Bay for his health. A bungalow was built for him on the cliff overlooking the beach. It is that low, Victorian style granite building at the turn of the beach road below the railway bridge, and is known as Cliff Cottage, although formerly it was The Nest. My mother used to call there to see Captain Josiah when she was a little girl. Weather permitting, he would lie on a bed-chair in the garden, and he enjoyed having visitors.

Carbis Bay Wesleyans had their own hymnist. He was Mr Thomas Ninnis Warmington of Longstone, a devoted member of the Boskerris congregation. I remember the carols he composed as Christmas favourites throughout Cornwall in his day, and they are still sung. His grandson is the famous St Ives artist, Mr Bryan Pearce.

The Wesleyan and New Connexion Chapels went each its separate way. Its congregation all turned up in go-to-meeting best, never attending the rival chapel. To each its own services, .harvest festivals, concerts, services of song, sewing meetings, Good Friday teas, outings - all those village activities that knit small communities into a caring whole which, if at times over-concerned with personal affairs, knew of everyone's troubles too and tended its members in sickness and affliction.

Chapel business was meticulously conducted, as you can see in the copper-plate accounts kept from 1901 to 1915. The handsome pages disclose prices which bear no relation to today's. Thus Mr E. Faull of St Ives charged £5. 5. 9 for six ceremonial trowels elegantly carved for the chapel's stone-laying ceremony of 1st March 1901 - postponed, an entry shows, for four days because of the weather. St Ives was further involved when its town crier was paid a shilling to proclaim the event around the district.

Here are the accounts for the Sunday School Prize Giving Tea of 12th January 1911.

Bailey's Bill	30 Buns	at 2½d	6.3	
	12lb Saffron Cake	4d	4.0	
	6lb Seed Cake	5d	2.6	
	6 doz. Splits	4d	2.0	
				14.9
Mrs Cowling	2lb Sweets		1.3	
	Oranges		1.6	
	2lb Butter		2.9	
				5.6
Mrs Frazier	2lb Sugar)			
	½ lb Tea)		1.4	
Miss Martin	Milk		10	
Chapel Keeper			1.0	
TOTAL				£1.3.5

In Sunday Best for the Chyangwheal New Connexion Methodists' Tea Treat
at Mr Williams's Picnic Grounds, probably in 1904.

The highlight of the year was the Choir Outing. The choir set forth in Jersey cars and go-to-meeting clothes to a mutually agreed venue, and a rare old time was had by all. People in those days had a capacity for group enjoyment that is not so evident now. Jersey cars were horse-drawn wagons with seats rising in tiers from front to rear. They were superseded by charabancs about 1920. Motive power apart, there was not all that difference between the two conveyances.

Tea treats - sometimes known as tea fights - were also a feature of the lighter side of chapel life. Arrived at the festal scene, each child was given a saffron bun as big as a plate. There were games and sports, and much eating. The Wesleyans patronised Mr Payne's Tea Gardens, Mr Payne being one of their flock. The Cottage Hotel is there today. The New Connexion Methodists favoured Mr Williams's Picnic Grounds further down the valley, Mr Williams being of course a Methodist. His house was the last in the valley, next to Carbis Bay hotel on the other side of the viaduct. The hotel came into being soon after the railway. It was built over mine workings at the very edge of the foreshore.

Just above the picnic grounds was Eden Cottage, the home of Mr Pearce the postman. Mr Pearce delivered the letters all round Carbis Bay, on foot, six days a week, twice daily. He found great satisfaction in his job, and said so. Outside his cottage gate was an extremely deep well from which the people in the lower valley fetched their water.

Not all the inhabitants of Carbis Bay belonged to these persistently independent chapel groups. There were the churchgoers. Until 1948 Carbis Bay was in the parish of Lelant, as St Ives had been five centuries earlier. It was run by the Parish Council and the West Penwith Rural District Council. St Uny Lelant being the parish church, most Carbis Bay residents, even the chapel people, were christened and married there, and buried in the churchyard above the Hayle estuary.

In 1910 Carbis Bay Anglicans got the use of the large room at Payne's and held Sunday services there. Then they built the little wooden church in Porthrepta Road. It is now a shop abutting the caravan park and ancient Little Gonwyn farmland. Opposite rose in due

course the beautiful Church of Saint Anta and All Saints, consecrated in 1929 and added to quite recently. An anonymous gift of £7,000 had started it on its way, while the granite blocks were given too. The belfry has a fine peal of bells, and the former vicar, Canon Roberts, is one of Cornwall's leading campanologists. The church began with a priest-in-charge and then became a parish church with a vicar of its own. As most of our churches are, it is conspicuously sited and enriches the landscape. The Croft, next door, was purchased to be the vicarage; and a splendid vicarage it is. Originally an artist's home, it was afterwards occupied by Mrs John Holman of the famous engineering firm in Camborne, and then by her daughter Mrs Rushbrook. A church hall has been added, and the church, reverting to the medieval function of its mother church, has become indispensable to Carbis Bay.

Particulars of the sale of Tyringham land name the purchasers of various tracts at Carbis Bay, among them Mr John Payne of the Valley Tea Gardens. John Payne, who bought the beach, and his son Jack who developed it, both played a considerable part in the establishment of Carbis Bay as a holiday centre. After the coming of the railway the next upheaval to hurry this group of hamlets into unity and modern times was the break-up and selling off, in 1920, of the Trevethoe Estate.

On the land John Payne bought from Squire Tyringham, and on an adjoining plot he acquired from Mr Lawry, he developed the Sunnyside Estate on the open space seaward of Chyangwheal. This was a significant step in the transformation of Carbis Bay into a residential suburb of St Ives, a transformation regretted no doubt by the older inhabitants but inevitable in the progression of the years. However, the glorious view of the bay was in no way obscured.

John Payne's other notable development in Carbis Bay was his tea gardens. They were originally sited on Little Gonwyn land, which his father William Payne farmed, on what is known today as Headland Road. By 1887 houses were under construction there. This was fifty years after Queen Victoria had ascended the throne, and the new road was appropriately named Jubilee Row. A scrap of history was concealed when the name was changed. But nine years previously John had abandoned the Little Gonwyn site and re-opened nearer the beach. I quote the Cornish Telegraph of 19th September 1878. Noting that the GWR had coined the name Carbis Bay for their station in Carbis Valley, and that the name was henceforward to apply to the whole area, the paragraph continues, "Carbis Valley is waking up. Visitors are being catered for with most obliging and economical readiness. Mr Payne is laying out the side of the hill in garden ground, and trying his best to convert a rough pasture of gorse and bracken into an ornamental tea garden."

John Payne's best efforts were rewarded. From what had been a most unpromising stretch of neglected mining land, "dumps" and all, he created what was to become within a few years a little valley of singular beauty, with every appearance of having been the gem of the region from time immemorial. Planting trees and shrubs and making winding paths down to the beach, he turned desolation into a leafy dell. He constructed his new tea gardens half-way down the valley. They were a paradise for children in an age when West Cornwall catered hardly at all for their amusement. Payne's Tea Gardens provided swings and seesaws and roundabouts, and shops selling lemonade and sweets, buckets and spades and whatever besides was needed for fun on the sands. They were a favourite venue for school treats and every sort of outing, and not only for the youngsters. Camborne and Redruth people arrived by the train load, or else along the gated roads across the North Cliffs by Jersey cars and such. The rail fare from St Ives was a penny for adults, a halfpenny for children; "Payne's" and the beach were just as popular with our St Ives neighbours. There were tea rooms, grottoes for the more discreet savouring of the cup - and the company - that cheers, and souvenirs in the shop. In the big room where the church services were first held John Payne laid down a fine maple floor. The room was therefore in demand for parties and dances; indeed it was the only place in Carbis Bay suitable for such festive occasions. The Tea Gardens were a haven of gaiety - Sundays excepted. They offered an enduring novelty and were besides a needful adjunct to the beach.

The coastal landlords had valued their beaches for the "right to wreck" they held thereby. The harvest of the sea was not all fish. Without such right stripping a wreck was wrecking - that notorious and illegal supplement to an inadequate income a Cornishman rarely rejected when it came his way. It was a Mr James of St Ives who, when the loveliest branch line in the West came into service in 1877, first realised the beach's potential as a holiday playground. Formerly known as either Porthrepta or Baripper, or Carrack Gladden Cove, it now shared with everywhere else in the neighbourhood the name the railway company had bestowed upon their station. Mr James rented the beach from Squire Tyringham. Photographs taken during the merrymaking years of Edward VII's reign show a row of bathing machines along the water's edge, a dozen or so tents above the tideline, huts from which he hired out bathing costumes and towels, and people so abundantly overdressed walking the sands.

Such sands too - soft and white and the better part of a mile from point to point, enclosed within gentle cliffs and with picturesque rocks at either end! Safe for bathing withal. Previously Porthrepta had been a minor fishing beach with bollards and several capstans beside the present hotel site which bespoke fishing boats moored there. Two or three little stone huts and upturned boats served as fishermen's shelters. There was also considerable mining activity thereabouts. But economic forces put an end to this, while the completion of station and viaduct ushered in a new prosperity. One last reversion to old times was attempted, however, between the wars, when a consortium sank an exploratory shaft at the foot of the valley. It was a fruitless effort.

Carbis river splashed out of the valley and wound its way across the sand to the sea, dividing the beach. On the St Ives side, towards Porthminster Point, was the old Providence mine. Its tumbledown engine house was recently demolished; it threatened to collapse on people on the beach below. Providence galleries ran far out under the sea. Further west, when the tide is low you can walk round to a minute cove beneath Penmester. It has its own mini-beach and a cave behind it. Formerly known as Zawn Abadden, the cove with the cave, it came to be called Couch's Cove after a boat owned by one of the Couches was wrecked there.

A spring tide at the ebb will allow you to walk on the

sands right round Hawkes Point to Porthkidney beach. You pass caves and tunnels, which are adits of East Providence mine and ran up to the mines at the back. Some of the adits have been blocked up for safety's sake; but in my young days every local boy at some time or other lit a candle in a jam jar and ventured as far into the land as he could go, rousing weird echoes and with tales of the "knockers" becoming more and more frighteningly real at every step, while rock face gleamed red and green under its watery film against the retreating darkness.

I remember how the roofs of the cave and adit entrances were festooned with clusters of maidenhair fern. Few have escaped uprooting, if not witless destruction. The clusters would cling to the cliff and hang as far up the cave as the north light could penetrate, the water from the rock trickling down through its delicate fronds and falling in pearly drops. Tear drops! The tears, they say, of a girl who loved to stroll, as we did, with her lover along the beach. One day she climbed the cliff path above the rocks to pick flowers while he bathed. She saw him swim through the breakers, and idled awhile among the sea pinks and heather and cliff-top blooms. Then she lay on the turf at the edge of the cliff, where there are many little hollows cherished by lovers, peeping over to watch for his return. Anxiety swelled to dreadful certainty. He had drowned. She wept and wept, staring through her tears at the relentless tide below, and weeping she died. The tears streamed down the maiden's hair, collecting in sad droplets at the tip of every tress, and they are streaming still.

THE LEGEND OF THE FERN

"Barepta sands are hot to tread,
    Cool, cool is the sea!
Climb the path to Gladden Head,
    Wait on the cliff for me,

Watch me dive and ride the surf
    And swim in the summer waves!
I'll join you, maid, on the soft sweet turf
    Atop the tinners' caves."

"I've climbed the path to the cliff above,
    I've watched you breast the sea
So vast, and you so little, love.
    O would you had stayed with me!"

On Carbis shore gaunt shadows glide,
    The shapes of the sea-rim reach
Close and close, as the creeping tide
    Covers an empty beach.

"Come back to me, my lover! Come!
    No more I'll let you go!
Out of the dusk the gulls drift home,
    The harbour lanterns glow."

She leant at the cliff's edge, called and cried
    And looked for her love's return;
Tears threading her long, loosed hair, she died -
    And a dewy, fairy fern

Swelled from the cliff where her hair had hung
    As she kept vigil there -
Grief's evergreen when I was young;
    We called it Maidenhair.

The Carbis Valley, about 1880. The house on the left is Glenside.
(Courtesy RIC)

CHAPTER VII

STORM, MINING AND SCHOOL

My mother used to tell me how once, when she was eight and a November gale which had been raging for two nights and a day was still battering the windows, my Great Uncle Henry took her down to the cliff top. They struggled down the grassy slope in front of Chyangwheal, crouching and battling against the wind, to look at three steamships, or what was left of them, that had been driven ashore on Carbis Bay beach all in one half-hour the previous day. Two were colliers - the *Cintra* of about 400 tons and the *Vulture* of 350 tons, both bound for Dartmouth. The third was the *Bessie* of nearly 300 tons, built nearby in Harvey's yard at Hayle; iron like the others but barquentine rigged, and Portland bound. The tide was out, and the plates of the *Cintra* were splayed in the middle of the beach. Next came the scrap heap that had been the *Vulture,* while the *Bessie,* still resembling a ship though with funnel and mainmast gone, lay under the cliff at Hawkes Point.

You can still walk or paddle around the remains of the three wrecks when the spring tide is at its lowest, though sometimes the sand is piled so deeply over them that they are out of sight for years. They lie there lost but not forgotten until some shift of current scoops half the beach across the bay to Gwithian during a wild winter, and there they are again.

The boilers of the *Vulture* were for long objects of curiosity to visitors and an "adventure playground" for children, until they went for scrap early in World War Two along with every railing and wrought iron gate in the district, not excluding the 160-year-old railings round Knill's Steeple. It is said that long after the war ended the railings of England, and presumably of Cornwall too, were still piled up in junk-yards and had better been left where they were.

There are various accounts of the "*Cintra* Gale". Shortly before he died at the age of 83 my father, an eye witness, recorded the terrible scene of seventy

years before. His memory was remarkably keen. Nightfall of November 16th, 1893, found the doomed steamers sheltering in St Ives Bay from a south-easterly gale, just as the trawler fleets do today. After a lull, before daybreak the hurricane burst forth again with redoubled fury, and veered to north'ard. Tremendous seas rolled in on the beaches. To avoid being driven ashore the ships which until then had lain safe and snug now had to up-anchor and get out to sea. They could not do it, though their desperate efforts continued well into the morning. Each towering wave would toss the bows high in the air as it rolled towards the shore, "pulling up chain, anchor and everything. Then down again," recalled my father. "So little time before the next sea came." Eventually *Bessie* and *Vulture* contrived to cut their cables, but they had by then dragged too close inshore. Their crews waved to each other across the turmoil of water as first the *Bessie,* and fifteen minutes later the *Vulture,* was dashed ashore on the beach. Rescuers were awaiting them, the breeches buoy apparatus had been rigged, the rockets were fired and the lifelines passed to the wrecks, and every man of both ships was hauled safely to land. The St Ives lifeboat had not been available. She was fighting the gale off Gwithian, where two fishing boats began to break up when the wind had veered. By now it was blowing so violently that it twice stopped the train approaching Carbis Bay station on the branch line.

Half an hour after the *Bessie* was wrecked the *Cintra,* too, was aground. She had waged a losing battle with the storm for much of the night, and had almost sunk at anchor. It was the anchor, in fact, that cost many lives. When at the first threat of a lee shore she prepared to slip her cable, a great sea swept the foc's'l, jamming the windlass and fouling the anchor. Every attempt to cut it loose was foiled by the rolling and pitching and the smother of green seas over her decks. The ship's lifeboat was lowered with four men in it. One account says that it capsized and that all four men were drowned, but my father declared that it drifted round to Porthkidney sands, where three of them were rescued. *Cintra,* meanwhile, with her anchor dragging all askew, hit the beach broadside on, the incoming waves thundering over the stranded vessel as if she were a half-tide breakwater. The crew climbed into the rigging, then jumped down on to the beach as each breaker receded, only to be sucked out by the undertow, some being "carried right under the bottom of the steamer and out to sea." In all thirteen were lost, my father recalled, but had they jumped into the advancing waves they would have been washed up into the hands of coastguards and others who were reaching to grab them.

In the afternoon *Vulture*'s mast gave way and "she fell abroad like a pack of cards." The *Cintra* too quickly disintegrated. The *Bessie,* built locally as father proudly insisted, lasted a lot longer. He watched the recovery of *Cintra*'s anchor in '59; it took him back sixty-six years.

Calamity had struck not only at Carbis Bay. The *Cintra* Gale wreaked great destruction at St Ives. At sea, while the three steamships were breaking up at Carbis Bay the 1000-tonner *Rosedale,* in ballast and so particularly responsive to the mighty pressure of the blast, was staggering up the coast bound for Cardiff. She made it round St Ives headland at midday and was driven broadside on to Porthminster Beach. The lifeboat, propelled by sails and oars in those days, and just back from Gwithian, came alongside but was cast up on the sands. However, the rocket party, which had rescued so many seamen earlier that day, again saved all hands. The breeches buoy apparatus, you know, was the invention of the Cornishman Henry Trengrouse of Helston.

The *Cintra* Gale had not done its worst, however. Soon after dark that dreadful November 17th, the 1600-ton *Hampton* foundered off Godrevy with but a solitary survivor.

The headland which had witnessed such distressing happenings that morning, and is known nowadays as Hawkes Point, is really two points. The one overlooking Carbis Bay is Carrack Gladden, "the rock on the brink". Hawkes Point is so called, I am told,

because hawks had always nested there in considerable numbers. It looks along Porthkidney sands to a hump where the little chapel of the Lelant Guild of St Anta stood before shifting sands swallowed it up. As for Porthkidney, this long, lovely stretch of white sand was "Porth Cunys" in Old Cornish, the firewood beach.

The cliff path on Carrack Gladden led until recently to a huers' hut, a whitewashed cob building which had to be demolished because through misuse it had become a public nuisance. This hut, commonly referred to in my father's day as a baulking house, used to be manned continuously from September to November. The huers had a skilled and responsible job. On spotting the glinting scales, or as often just a dark patch in the sea that only experience could interpret as millions of pilchards, they would signal across the bay to St Ives and the other baulking house where today you sit to catch your breath after climbing up from Porthminster Beach. The iron bridge over the railway line was erected for the huers' convenience.

The path runs round the edge of the cliff to Hawkes Point, then down steps to Porthkidney, and there in the rock is the entrance to a mine. Once known, quite delightfully, as the "Fanny Adela", it was worked by half a dozen miners for its copper pyrites, but it was "knacked" along with all the rest. A gateway where you cross the railway line for the beach leads to Hawkes Point Cottage. Mr and Mrs Edward Ashton occupied it in the late 1800s and reopened the Fanny Adela as Hawkes Point Mine, but professionals reckoned that it contained "too much of everything and too little of anything to make it a *keenly bal"* - that there were so many different ores in the mine that it was too costly to separate out the various metals. So in due course the Ashtons had to accept the inevitable. Mrs Ashton, who was a woman of remarkable force of character, went down to the workings herself. With her own hands she dislodged some of the timber props, causing the "ground" to cave in and thereby sealing the mine.

The Ashtons had better luck when they laid out some very pretty tea gardens around the cottage. Walkers would stop there for splits and cream, saffron cake and tea, then go on through the Nut Grove to the Wishing Well. Venton Uny, or the Fairies' Well, was revered ages before the landing of the saints. You approach it down a steep track which branches off from the main path beneath the hazel trees. It is poised near the brink of the cliff. Unlike many other Cornish holy wells promoted to shrines when the church could not stop its flock from frequenting them, it has no cover save the entwining boughs. However, a white stone grotto stood at the verge nearby; it disappeared during the last war. The well's fairy function is acknowledged today by romantic young couples who still wander hand in hand over West Cornwall, bless them! despite the un-romance of shabby jeans and the let's-get-on-with-it attitude of their generation, and even by passers-by who are neither young nor couples. They wish while dropping bent pins into the trough from which water flows to tumble in a tiny waterfall to the sea.

What a desolate spot it used to be, right out on the point! When I was eight and World War One was at its height, I was climbing the rocks there with a cousin when we found a store of petrol cans in a cave. For some reason we felt we had stumbled on something we should not see - really afraid, we were! - and we ran away. It is a poignant memory. Now I look back and wonder.

Mr Ashton was a photographic artist, a pioneer of natural as distinct from the studio photography which the late Victorians preferred. His discerning studies reveal the charm and tell the story of old St Ives. Mrs Ashton had the healing touch and was to become known far beyond the bounds of Penwith and even of Tamar as "Granny Ashton". In 1933, not long before she died, she declared her intention to give the town a section of coastline at Hawkes Point, together with the Nut Grove, St Uny's Well and the Grotto. Mr W. C. T. Tregarthen, the author, in a letter from South Africa cites Mrs Ashton for the information that Hawkes Point was once overrun with rabbits. It was originally attached to the Trevethoe Estate and the squire used the cottage as a shooting lodge. "On the authority of the late Mrs Ashton," he continues, "it will be of value to record that it was in this isolated nook that the Cornish antiquary William Botterell, an old Celt, wrote his two unique volumes of <u>Traditions and Hearthside Stories of West Cornwall</u>, published in 1870 and 1873."

Carbis Bay Beach road leads steeply up over the railway bridge to Longstone, along Porthrepta Road. On the right, just below the church, is Hendra's Hotel. This hotel, then Hendra's Restaurant, was advertised in 1896 as "Ten minutes' walk from the Show Grounds", the Royal Cornwall Agricultural Show for the year being held at Trelyon. 1987 marked the centenary of the hotel, which had remained with Mrs Hendra's family all those years and was well known to generations of holidaymakers.

Carbis Bay Hotel was also early on the scene, after the Great Western Railway had cut its way across Hawkes Point and, stopping at the station below Mr Begbie's house, continued over the graceful viaduct and round the bend to St Ives. Mr Harold Begbie was a best-selling author. His house, Bosahan, with considerable additions is now St Uny Hotel.

Carbis Bay Hotel added a lot to the accommodation available at Carbis Bay for summer visitors at the close of the last century. At the time of the Royal Cornwall Show here there were otherwise only five sitting rooms, with fifteen bedrooms and twenty-one beds, to let. This would indicate that apartments were on offer at only five private houses. What a difference today! Thus did tourism catch up on Carbis Bay.

Little Gonwyn Farm was opposite Hendra's Hotel. Part of the farmhouse still is, though you would hardly recognise it as today's modern dwelling. At the top of the hill, turning towards St Ives along the main road you come to Boskerris Lane, beside the Atlantic Hotel. This lane led to the two Boskerris farms, Woolas and Wartha, each with its farmhouse and outbuildings of granite. Between them they farmed all the fields to the main road and across it right down to the station. They had to fetch their drinking water from a well at the bottom of the lane. At the side was a cattle trough. Boskerris land was good land, and the hedges along the lane were full of the wild flowers Cornwall offers in such profusion. The views seaward, and up to Knill's Steeple, were arresting, but now all has disappeared under a growth of houses and bungalows. Even the trough has gone, while you would never know where the well had been. It was at Boskerris, I would remind you, that Mary Behenna, the mother of the actor Sir Henry Irving, was reared.

Carbis Bay, soon after the arrival of the railway (1877)

Continuing on from Boskerris fields brings us into what was in my young days a dereliction of mine workings. Providence and Wheal Speed mines had been great in their time. You reached them up Count House Lane in Chyangwheal, that hamlet where I spent so much of my childhood and which grew up around Providence Mine in the 1700s. The lane leads off the main road between Idris and my Great Uncle William's house, which he built just before 1900 and named Bay View. Following his death in 1908 Great Aunt Mary lived there for many years. Communications between the house on the right and the house on the left of the lane were not all they might have been, owing to a family quarrel which went on and on and seemed likely to last for ever. But that's village life for you!

The first turning towards St Ives leads to Chyangwheal Farm, former home of the veteran Jameson raider. The old Count House further up Count House Lane is much as it was in days gone by. The late Mr Bernard Leach, world-renowned potter, lived here with his family for many years. His daughter has the Count House now. Not only was the office work and the accounting done at the Account (now the Count) House. Shareholders held their quarterly meetings there, and, business over, sat down to a sumptuous meal prepared by the staff and no doubt followed by hearty junketing. These Count House dinners were common in Cornish mining circles. Many of the mines sported their own stamped china for the occasion; you can see fine specimens in Truro Museum, each bearing the name of the mine. Botallack at Pendeen dined its shareholders as at the Lord Mayor's banquet; it used a dinner service made from its own tin and polished until it shone like silver. What can have become of it?

Wheal Providence and Wheal Speed workings sprawled opposite the Count House. They had long been derelict when I was a child, and were a real adventure playground. Crumbling walls and relics, shallow troughs now aswarm with frogs, newts and tadpoles, hollows left when the massive machinery was removed to become boating ponds, filled wondrous hours. As at Consols on Good Friday the local boys would sail anything on Wheel Speed pond from model yachts to "corken barbers". These were made from the chunks of cork that supported the drift nets or, with a

pole stuck through the middle of a pile of them, served as marker buoys. You broke or cut one of them in half, roughly shaped it with a knife, and finished off the job by rubbing it against that part of a granite wall which you had secretly discovered to possess outstanding abrasive qualities, and with a sliver of slate for a keel and sails of seagull quills or wood chips trimmed to the wind, how bravely your ship reached America on the far side of the pond!

The workings lay immediately behind Idris; come to think of it I never in all my life recall hearing Great Aunts Mary Anne and Elizabeth discussing the tin mine at their back door. Their concern was all for chapel and the view seaward. Wheal Providence workings were not so extensive as you might imagine. They were a concentration of granite buildings and sheds and great waste dumps in not such a wide area. The vast extent of the mines was underground. The galleries followed the tin and copper lodes down to the beach; you can see Providence adits there with the water they drained off trickling into the sand. Deeper still the miners had tunnelled, level with the sea-bed and then, as with Wheal Margery, deeper and deeper yet and under the sea, the introduction of steam machinery having enabled the adequate drainage of the lowest levels. But now the depths were silent, as up top I played among the ruins. Furze and brambles concealed decay beneath a blanketing tangle, ivy crept up tumbling walls and grass carpeted the ground, but not everywhere. There were large patches of red, clayey soil where nothing would grow, while the dumps were but sparsely covered. For among the waste brought up from virgin rock below were chemicals inimical to vegetation.

You cannot exactly date the beginnings of these Carbis Bay mines. Among "Tynnworkes of name" the Elizabethan topographer John Norden lists in 1584 is "Carbisse, in St Ies". Wheal Providence's earliest production figures were given in the 1757-9 accounts, when a small quantity of copper ore was raised and sold. Up to then, by the way, Providence had been known as Tregozy mine. Carbis Bay was mainly a source of tin, copper being found only in small pockets.

The mines were closed down, as they were being closed

Wheal Providence, probably in the late 1870s after the mine closed
(Courtesy RIC)

all over Cornwall, in 1878-9. The declining price of tin in the world market, and the increasing cost of production as the mines ran deeper, rendered them uneconomical. Huge quantities of alluvial tin and cheap labour abundantly available were being exploited in the Far East. It had just to be shovelled and streamed, as in those oft-told days when, it was said, the miners of Penwith worked the river beds and dug shallow trenches and carried the bright metal along the Hayle River, through St Erth and so to the Phoenician traders at Ictis, St Michael's Mount to be. Many ancient tin routes led to Hayle to start the journey to the biblical lands. But now, after countless generations had mined the hard rock, the Cornish miners faced destitution. They had worked in small, independent groups of "tributers", under contract to the management; and now there were no contracts on offer. It was the Great Depression. However, throughout the nineteenth century and into the twentieth, gold was being discovered in faraway parts of the world - California, Australia, South Africa, the Yukon. There was silver in South Africa, diamonds at Kimberley. And wherever there was metal to be dug, and hard rock to drill, there the Cornish miners flocked. It was said that wherever there was a hole in the ground, you would find a Cornishman at the bottom of it. Contemporary newspapers display advertisements for cheap passages by sea and sail to the ends of the earth: so our young men left home with their sepia photographs of loved ones to be thumbed out of recognition until success - and they often made big money - or failure brought them back to Cornwall, too often with only an agonised year or two to live because of the dreaded miners' disease. Most of them got back, though we all know families some member of whom sailed away never to be seen or heard of again. In every country you can think of where gold or silver was mined you will find to this day Cornish communities living in the Cornish style, proper pasties, saffron cake, chapel teas and all. While the wanderer was away most mothers and wives could confidently expect a monthly wage packet, to be opened under the tense gaze of the sender's likeness on mantelpiece or what-not, as he posed in the unaccustomed and ill-fitting suit in which he had set out on his adventures.

Forced by circumstances into two quite separate existences, the Cornish miner - "Cousin Jack" - was paradoxically apt to be both parochial and man-of-the-world at the same time. Thus a miner returned from abroad could observe, "London - what do 'ee want to go there for? Too far for me, booy - never been no further than Truro. 'Ess, I been to Africa and America, but 'tedn' the same, an it?"

A distinction of another sort is illustrated in a story my father recorded during his last illness. Two old miners meet after chapel. "Sorry to hear Jan's died." "Naw, 'e didn' die. 'E was kilt." "'Ow's 'at, ah?" "'E went up shaft. Stanked 'pon plank. Plank wasn't there. Fell down shaft, plank an' all. So 'e was kilt." "Aw, now I do knaw."

Two large shafts behind Idris, each descending beside its own engine house, were known as Higgs' shaft and Hawk's shaft. Both have been filled in. The Higgs engine house was bulldozed down into the shaft in a single morning - such a noble structure when contrasted with today's tile and concrete! - when the building estate which has smothered the area was begun. The red mine dump that was a landmark to generations of Carbis Bay people was dispersed over the surrounding ground in as brief a time. Strange to say, though precious little would ever grow on the mound the dozens of gardens around bloom beautifully on the tainted soil! But how changed it all is from when, many years ago, we took our small son to play where mother had played, called the ivied ruin by the mound the Giant's Castle, and told him the wonderful tales of giants and piskeys that belong to West Cornwall! When he returns from "Down Under" and takes his own sons to the beloved spot he is in for a sad surprise.

These old mines used to be the haunts, I am told, of piskeys and spriggans and knockers, and even of Old Bucca himself coming in from the sea on his day, or night, off. Bucca, you must know, was one of the minor gods in the bay whom our fishing ancestors held in deep respect, and whom they bore fearfully in mind long after the saints had moved in to achieve by supplication what the offspring of the Titans had to be persuaded to do by ceremony, offerings and appropriate gestures.

St Ives Consols, photographed by Gibson in about 1863.
Notice that the workforce includes children. (Courtesy RIC)

Professor Hunt, who knew all about these things, explains that piskeys were mischievous fairies - Puck-like individuals; that spriggans resided wherever you found cairns or cromlechs and coits and barrows, and though he did not mention ruined mines you may be sure they were there too: you meddled with them at your peril; knockers you can still hear tapping away underground if you listen beside a shaft: they are the souls of Jews who formerly, it was believed, worked the tin mines of Cornwall. Knockers were also known as buccas, though as mentioned Old Bucca was spoken of as a sea god too. He certainly got around! My old aunts' firm belief in piskeys and spriggans was shared by most of their generation; so much happened about the place for which there was no other explanation. I think that Cornish hearts today, albeit we would never confess it, still cherish the belief, though we no longer leave bits of pasty and fuggan (cake) around to appease the little fellows and avoid ill-wishing. Perhaps we know them today as "little green men" - which, if you think of it, is what they always have been! I suspect, though, that the knockers of the mines were bats, who occupied the mouths of shafts since capped - to account in part for the dearth of bats which once executed amazing aerobatics above our gardens at dusk.

A left turn just above the mine on the skyline brings you to the very early hamlet of Carninney. With that delightful freedom in spelling common to all ages but our own, the place was Karneny in 1327, Carneny in 1365, Carnyny in 1391, Carninie in 1649 and Carneney in 1659. Carn, a heap of rock, is common in Cornish place-names, but otherwise the significance of the name has not been traced. It seems that a cattle pound was established there in 1552, but there is no sign of it now. For all that, Carninney is singularly unchanged. I have always felt that a walk to Carninney took me right into the past, hundreds of years back. Two old farm houses are there and a long, sunken lane runs alongside. I should hate to see it swallowed up by yet another building estate.

On Worvas Downs between Carninney and Knill's Steeple is a quaint house formerly called Heath Cottage but now modernised, Little Wheal Speed. It enjoys the most beautiful views of St Ives Bay, while in the back garden is a small amphitheatre, a miniature Gwennap Pit, which has served in turn as a smelting pit, a place of worship and a cockpit when cock fighting survived in out-of-the-way spots. It is about sixty feet in diameter, and the preacher's stone is there still.

A Miss Penberthy lived in Heath Cottage, as had generations of her family before her. I knew her as one of the elderly visitors who used to drop in at my aunts' for a dish o' tay and a slice of saffron cake on the long haul home from shopping in St Ives. In her prime she had been, they say, quite magnificent. She was renowned as having crossed the Atlantic neither for need nor for duty but simply to visit the Chicago World Fair; though what she thought of this breathtaking exhibition I never heard tell. Her Christian names were Mary Anna and as such she was known. But not by me. When I was very small she put me firmly in my place. "I am Miss Penberthy to you." I never forgot, as you can see. She, like all my great aunts, carried a walking stick. Mary Anna lived in her Heath Cottage to a great age, and so did her mother before her. A noisy, vicious dog guarded her front door.

What a backcloth to Carbis Bay those rhododendrons were, that covered Worvas Hill all the way up to the Steeple-crowned summit! What a sight when they were in bloom! They are splendid still, but much fewer. Under the bushes and the trees of Tregenna Woods you can find the "old men's workings", shallow excavations made long, long ago when you could get tin just by digging a ditch for it. Aunt Elizabeth and I loved to walk across the gorse-grown desolation of Wheal Speed, an eruption of pure gold in springtime, and up through the rhododendrons to Knill's. On the way we would sit down to rest on a patch of camomile grass. The haunting scent of it lingers in memory, for it lingers nowhere else. There Aunt Elizabeth would tell me, as her sister did beside the great big bed, those tales of piskeys and their kind which were so real to her, and to me too at the time, never frightening and mostly amusing. Ancient, pagan Cornwall peeped through the chapel trappings of even so staunch a Methodist as she.

Over the brow of the hill by Knill's Steeple and we were back at Halsetown. My mother told me how one day, for fun, she and other young people went to Halsetown Fair. There they had their fortunes told by an old crone called Kitty Hunkin who was renowned for unveiling the secrets of the future. The girls had to walk home across the Steeple after nightfall, and Kitty Hunkin had told their fortunes in such lurid detail that they were terrified and fearful of passing every bush. I suspect Kitty knew what she was about! Lelant also held a fair in those days, while Fair Mo - or Fairy Mo - at St Ives was another attraction for youngsters. It was the done thing to bring back fairings for those who stayed at home. I remember a bag of fairings to have contained ginger nuts, macaroons and sugar almonds. Hamlyn's, whose cake shop at St Ives was patronised from far and wide, sold the best fairings and had stalls at the fairs. It is a Chinese restaurant now. What with the fairs, and chapel events, guise dancing, carols and concerts at Christmas, Christmas parties and birthday parties, brass bands, and, of course, the major occasion of the year, the circus, life at Carbis Bay was gay enough.

I suppose we seem to have been rather simple by today's standards. Lacking all modern "props" of entertainment we relied the more on imagination, an invaluable but I fear diminishing asset and a certain antidote to boredom. However rich life in big cities was, in the country we had got to make our own amusement. The cinema was in its infancy when I was in mine. The nearest we got to it in Carbis Bay then was the magic lantern. This marvel of illusion threw pictures on to a sheet and was in great demand for chapel evenings, though possession of a magic lantern at home was vouchsafed only to the privileged few. The smell of burning oil and hot enamel from the lantern was a feature of a very special occasion. We would watch fascinated as the pictures hung in the dark before our eyes, and the lecturer indicated with his pointer those features of Nazareth or the Wailing Wall or a Bedouin encampment which deserved his comment.

We had to wait until the early '20s for radio, even though it was only a few miles south of us, at Poldhu on the Lizard, that Marconi had flashed that first signal across the Atlantic. While ear-phoned relations in London clustered mutely round crystal and "cat's whisker", we so remote from the broadcasting station had to make do with Mr Garbutt's arresting but frustrating lecture on the wonders of the "wireless". Wire-less? Soon, in a room on Skidden Hill, a room festooned with wires as thick as cobwebs in a Transylvanian castle, a few were listening to alarming atmospherics as their host manipulated knobs and flitted from battery jar to battery jar tightening and adjusting. Yes, he often got 2LO - but not then! Early radio was like that. It was years before it displaced the gramophone as the teenagers' delight.

Until recently there was no school at Carbis Bay. In my earliest schooldays Carbis Bay children had to walk to St Ives for their schooling, or to Trevarrack or Lelant, just as formerly Shanks's pony had taken them to "Passon" for such instruction as he found time to bestow. When I was five I went to Miss Cole's school in Porthminster Terrace. This was one of several private schools, Dames' Schools, to which with the Board School and the National School Carbis Bay kids tramped, fair weather and foul, five days a week. We mites carried a little satchel on our backs containing sandwiches or a pasty, and a tin of cocoa for washing them down at lunch. It was two miles there and two miles back from Chyangwheal. Older girls came from as far afield as Nancledra and Vorvas. One of them brought her cocoa ready made in a thermos flask. How I coveted it! Mother bought me one but I dropped it. Back to the tin!

During the First World War we rarely saw sweets or luxuries, but on one occasion, doubtless to commemorate some victory or other, no less a dignitary than His Worship the Mayor of St Ives, Mr Tom Uren, turned up at the school. He gave each one of us a little bag of boiled sweets. Mr Uren was slim and tall, and I remember to this day looking up at his, to me, great height and thinking what a wonderful man he was. Thereafter he was always a favourite of mine.

Although there was no bus service, public or otherwise, to take us to school, after 1877 there was the train. But the station was a longish step from the main road, and I suppose parents thought their children might as well walk the whole way as they had done since there were schools to walk to. Besides foot-sloggers along the St Ives road, horses, cobs and ponies and donkeys, and whatever wheeled contraptions they could be made to take in tow, clip-clopped and rumbled to and from town. Once a week horse-drawn vans delivered meat and groceries and all your other orders from St Ives: no lugging anything heavier than a parcel or two home yourself in those unenlightened times! Troachers trundled slowly by chanting their wares, fish and vegetables mostly. The last of these colourful characters, whom I used to know as the "pear boy", patrolled the road right up to recent years.

Between the 1914-18 war and the beginning of the next in 1939 everything came to Carbis Bay. The CMT bus service, forerunner of the Western National, reached these distant parts. Water, which previously we had had to pump to the top of the house, now gurgled into the cistern of its own accord. Gas and electricity were laid on. Many new houses were built; and Carbis Bay, no longer three clearly distinguishable villages, was becoming a single unit. This unification was completed with the dedication of St Anta and then its consecration as parish church of Carbis Bay. So had its mother church been consecrated eight hundred years before at Lelant. And that is another story.

At Trevethoe House, 1937.
On the front row, from left to right, are: the Lelant Beauty Queen; Mrs Tyringham; Ald. W. P. Toy, Daphne Toy and Mrs Toy (Lena's father, sister and mother); on her left is Squire Tyringham; and on the far right is the Carbis Bay Beauty Queen.

CHAPTER VIII

LELANT - CHURCH AND PARISH

Off to Lelant! Though there was one time when you could not have gone a step beyond Carbis Bay. That was just within living memory, when the Great Blizzard hit the whole South West. The snow came suddenly, following a week of unsettled weather and a wet Sunday, early in March 1891. It came in the clutch of a hurricane that blew people flat in the street, had cattle shuffling backwards into the cowshed since even they could not face the blast, buried flocks and herds and travellers, piled up the snow into impassable drifts. Wild winds sharp with freezing spray drove a ship ashore on Hayle bar, wild seas prevented the launching of the lifeboat, so the rocket-crew set out with their wagon-load of equipment by road. They got no further than Carbis Bay; a massive drift baulked their furious efforts to get through. Lelant was similarly blocked by a barrier of snow 200 yards long and nine feet deep. Here a local mine captain dug out a wagonette, its four horses, four girl passengers and the driver, and led them to shelter in the Praed Arms. The blizzard raged on and off for a week. In far Penwith we missed the worst of it, but what we got was enough!

Snow seldom more than brushes its frosty fingers across our countryside. As I have told you, I was fourteen before I saw snow save at a long distance. So you may expect a clear if sometimes wet and windy progress into the eastern limits of Greater St Ives. At the crossroads half way down Longstone Hill, the right hand lane was where the spectral coach was wont to ply when there was moonshining at the Wink and Wink Town must be prevailed upon to hide its head under the blankets. The road to the left leads round to the church, and as it turns along the golf links you are at the drive up to Gonwin Farm. Under a diversity of spelling "gon" means croft and "win" white: the White Croft. It was rebuilt on the old site as a farmhouse in Victorian days and the Wearns farm Gonwin now. Formerly it had been the ancestral home of the Pawleys, but the Gonwin Pawleys have died out. The

family stood in little fear of extinction in 1635, the slate tablet in Lelant church showing, besides "Stephen Pawley of this Parish Gentleman", his wife, five sons and six daughters, all in bas-relief. Another monument nearly eighty years later names seven children.

Gonwin was the "big house". Other dwellings and a smithy were on the estate. This stretched from the borders of Trevethoe to the cliff, where the Nut Grove, the Wishing Well and the slate quarry under the iron footbridge are and the grotto was. The quarry used to be carpeted with primroses, but they are fewer now, and the glow-worms once glittering there to mirror the stars are gone. Gunwyns too lived in the old house for several generations, being related to the Pawleys by marriage. They, their ancestors and others presumably servants are named in a row with the church in 1516, when "the inhabiters of the house called Gungwin" claimed exemption from mortuary fees.

The last of the Pawleys of Gonwin was a Miss Jane Pawley. She inherited the house and "some other remnants" of the estate. But, says Joseph Polsue in his Parochial History, "misfortunes and disreputable conduct reduced her to the extremity of soliciting alms from those who had once looked up to her, when she held a superior position; and this representative of an ancient family died in the poorhouse." Poor Jane! Our Victorian forebears, disposed to equate poverty with sin, were over-ready to condemn the unfortunate. It could not have been easy to maintain one's dignity when a vast, ancient dwelling was tumbling about one's ears and one had no means to maintain it. I imagine Miss Jane sharing a bottle in her dilapidated kitchen with a greasy couple who were all the company left to her; deserted when the drink and the wages ran dry; evicted; crushed and humiliated by charity; borne to a pauper's grave. Likely enough that is just what happened; a dismal end to a long and distinguished line.

Along the road, then, to the church. I was married there; in its churchyard lie many of my people, close to one of the two crosses that were there in Uny's time, and also across the footpath in the new, though not the newest, churchyard, while others are in that one too. The story of Lelant is very much that of the folk who rest in the shadow of its warm, four-square granite. Throughout its fifteen hundred years of history Lelant is documented as Lananta - "lan" the church and "nant" the valley. Though what valley is not clear. I prefer Canon G. H. Doble's interpretation. In his little book about the church he makes "lan" a monastery and "Anta" the founding saint. Nevertheless, the church was dedicated to St Uny (or Euny), said by William of Worcester to have been buried there. Anta as patron saint of Carbis Bay had to wait a whole millenium and a half for the dedication which you may consider her due. You can see her next to her sister Saint Ia in the Tyringham window above the altar at Lelant.

Fifth and sixth century Cornwall, the canon tells us, swarmed with monasteries established by monks from South Wales; the clerical settlers, as it were, who trod in the pioneering footsteps of the Irish missionaries. Canon Doble, though, doubts whether the saints of Penwith were Irish at all, but lacking proof to the contrary, we still look to the communal hermitages in the Wicklow Mountains - O wonderful Glendalough! - as their Alma Mater. Such vandals, those reforming clerics who destroyed the records of our saints, so that even the highest authority this side of Eden denies their existence! It seems that the scraps we know about them derive mainly from Welsh, German and French manuscripts. But even this scant confirmation is denied St Uny. We know him as Ia's brother, a member of that holy group who had dared the perilous Celtic Sea with Prince Fingar in boats of skins. Uny is the patron, too, of Redruth parish church while at Wendron, near Helston, was once a shrine to mark the place where he was martyred: Merther (murder of) Uny - today Marooney.

It is a little disconcerting that Dr Dexter, in the course of disproving around 1930 the Christian origins of various Cornish crosses, considers Uny to be female and identifiable with the Etruscan goddess Uni and Roman Juno. He argues that the goddess was promoted to sainthood by the early church, with a sex

change, when easing the Cornish out of paganism and into Christianity. If only the record of St Uny, written on imperishable parchment in round monkish script, had survived the Reformation! Still, we accept in faith what we presume our ancestors knew as fact. You will never shake a Cornishman's belief in his saints!

The parish of Uny Lelant included St Ives up to 1434 (and the benefice of St Ives till as recently as 1826) and Carbis Bay until 1948. At the Conquest it was part of the great manor of Ludgvan Leaze. William the Conqueror gave this manor to his half brother Robert Earl of Mortain, Lord of so much of Cornwall, and the de Cardinan family held it of the earl. The de Cardinans had built a castle at Cardinham, near Bodmin, while at Tywardreath by Par they founded a Benedictine priory. To this priory they granted, and confirmed the grant in 1150, "the church of Saint Uny, with the lands, tithes and other things belonging to it, in particular the village which is called Lananta and Tredrait, and the half acre of land in Hendra." Tredrait is the ancient seaport of Tredreath in lower Lelant. The half acre had been misappropriated by the Trembethows who lived under Trencrom Hill, but through threat of eternal torment the church got it back. The immortal Thomas a Becket, Archbishop of Canterbury, himself ratified the grant twenty years later.

At that time the living of Lelant was a rectory. In 1272 Bishop Bronscombe - he who transfigured the architecture of Exeter Cathedral from stolid Norman to soaring Gothic - transferred the benefice of Lelant to the Collegiate Church at Crediton which squeezed a fat £76 revenue out of the deal. However, he retained to himself and his successors the appointment of the parish priest, henceforward a vicar. We find the Precentor and Canons of Crediton the beneficiaries of an agreement made by Bishop Lacy, who after twenty years of sturdy opposition by the vicar of Lelant to a parish of St Ives had consecrated the new church of St Ia. The tithe of fish landed by St Ives and Lelant fishermen on the "Coner and Rayver sond" - Upton and Riviere Towans - was to go to Crediton. Hardly fresh fish when it got to the reverend collegiates!

A tribute of another sort had to be paid by St Ives worshippers to the mother church. Each Easter Day they brought a two-pound wax "candle of St Ya" to High Mass at Lelant church. Other offerings of candles and bread had to be made throughout the year, together with £1. 6s. 8d in cash. In the fullness of time King Henry VIII, dispossessing the Collegiate Church, seized the rectoral tithes of Lelant and sold them to a layman, fish and all. In 1533 Queen Mary, in restoring England to the Catholic faith for the brief period of her reign, returned to Uny Lelant "3 chalices and patens, 38 oz. and a pix of silver 4½oz."

The church plate in our times too seems to have endured adventurously. Canon Doble lists (1939) the Communion Plate, which "consists of 1 large Silver Flagon with this Inscription, *The Gift of Sir Nathll: Napier Bart: and Thomas Hearle Esqr: to the Parish of Lelant 1726* weight 55 oz." A silver salver and a silver chalice and cover were also scheduled. Now about twenty years ago a Mr Napier, a Scotsman resident at Pentre, Lelant - where incidentally the Tyringhams had lived for a time - returned home to find an old box in his hall and the door, in those key-free days, unbolted. It had been found in the vaults of Barclays Bank during reconstruction and contained the church plate, sent to Pentre because of the name on the flagon! But how it had got to the bank in the first place, or which of the large and ennobled Scottish family of Napiers our Mr Napier belonged to was a Sir Nathaniel, Baronet, in 1726, he had no idea. Equally baffling was what Sir Nathaniel was doing at Lelant, so long ago, and what his connection with Thomas Hearle Esquire of Lelant could have been, that they should jointly donate such valuable plate to the parish church. Had the Scotsman been shipwrecked off Lelant; had Mr Hearle sheltered him? All was and is conjecture, for the family archives in Scotland have been destroyed by fire. Of course, Mr Napier passed on his windfall to the vicar. One day, I suppose, the riddle will be solved.

Lelant suffered, sometimes scandalously, from absentee vicars. The Rev. James Gentell, vicar from 1505 to 1546, must have been an impressive and most competent clergyman, for he had been appointed Provost of Glasney, the great Collegiate Church at Penryn, and held the post up to its dissolution. He would have been well occupied with the affairs of the College in that difficult period, shorn though it had been of its monastic properties. Nevertheless, Gentell turned up at Lelant to sue parishioners for mortuary fees, the Gunwyns of Gonwin among them.

In 1549 Gabriel Morton, Vicar of Lelant, joined in the Prayer Book Rebellion. When the attempts of the rebel army to capture Exeter failed, he was captured and handed over to the fiendish Provost Marshal, Anthony Kingston, for judgement. But unlike John Payne, Portreeve of St Ives, whom you will recall Kingston sent to the gallows after first accepting his hospitality, and unlike several other rebel priests, one of them a Cornish namesake, Morton was not hanged. Instead Kingston made over all the wretched vicar's tithes and the fruits of his living - and we have seen that the revenues of medieval Lelant were considerable - to a Boscastle landowner, who enjoyed them until Queen Mary's time. Doubtless, being the man he was, Kingston enjoyed them too, while deprived of his livelihood Lelant's vicar could in no way have served his parish.

Things got really bad after the Reformation, which by destroying chantries and other pious foundations reduced the ranks of the clergy. The vicars of Lelant had St Ives to look after till 1836, and Towednack till 1901, as well as Lelant. This by no means impeded their acceptance of other benefices. Meanwhile at St Ives, stalls crumbled into decay while whitewashing the oak of the roof did nothing to dispel a general air of dilapidation. How different from today! In 1745 the Vicar of Lelant was living at St Ives, in 1779 at St Erth, where he was curate. In 1812 we find Cornelius Cardew, Rector of St Erme near Truro, Vicar of Lelant, living at St Erme when not performing his duties as Master of Truro Grammar School. He left it to his curate to serve the three parishes. It was a period when to the Anglican clergy enthusiasm was akin to idolatry, and enthusiastic about their spiritual mission they certainly were not. Small wonder that Methodism gained such a hold, nowhere more so than in the far South West!

Some of the neglect at Lelant, though, stemmed from the lack of a vicarage. At one time twenty acres of glebe, hedged and cultivated, which had accrued in the age of the saints, spread with thirty acres of commonland right down to the sea. St Uny Church stood among the fields. On Annyer Rock was a little chapel which showed a light for shipping entering the estuary. The vicarage was in the vicinity. Below the church was Churchtown - or so one would assume, this almost invariable term for a Cornish village nestling today beside its church being lacking at Lelant; while the pathway past the church, across the links and under the railway bridge to the foreshore, is recognisable as a village street with cottages either side. Lower down was a graveyard. When the railway cutting was dug, skeletons were found in walled graves.

What had happened to change Lelant Churchtown from a busy little seaport to sand dunes or as we would say, towans? First of course, the silting up of the estuary transferred the commercial activity to St Ives; second and much later, when the Archdeacon of Cornwall made his visitation to Uny Lelant in 1700 the churchwardens "Presented" to him "the Church, part wherof being fallen, and the churchyard and Viccaredge house ruinous - occasioned by the sands blown up from the sea, and wee have nothing else to present." The glebe lands disappeared under the sand, the further shifting of which has been forestalled by the planting of "bent grass", a rush which spreads readily over sea sand and binds the surface in a mesh of roots. As for the presumed Churchtown, Polsue records the tradition that "a town of some magnitude, having a market and custom house, stood near the church, when the river Hayle afforded deep water without the aid of engineering skill, and before St Ives had risen in importance. Foundations of houses have certainly been discovered under the sand." Within the glebe had been tin mines and these vanished too; you can see their adits beneath the point. The little chapel, Chapel Angier, went the way of St Piran's Oratory at Perranzabuloe and Gwithian Church near Godrevy - also under the sand.

Chapel Angier had been built in 1500 by the Guild of St Anta. The fifteen members of the fraternity and their successors had· been authorised by the vicar to "enjoy and possess in future all the oblations, both the greater and the lesser, made in the said chapel .... for the use of the fraternity of the chapel, provided that the aforesaid parishioners and brethren of the said fraternity shall repair, keep up, and if necessary

rebuild it at their own cost. There shall be paid annually to the aforesaid .... Vicar and his successors 6/8." But it never was rebuilt, and it would puzzle you to find what remains of it in the towans. The sea made a heavy onslaught in 1977-8, washing a great deal of the towans away on the Hayle side of the estuary and threatening buildings at the old ferry. But the chapel is on its rock and the sand firm on top of it; and for sure the Lelant folk who witnessed the sand storm so long ago saw the last of it. In 1978, though, a stout wall was built to save the buildings at the ferry from the sea. Sea and sand! The whole story of Lelant, its growth, its potential, its decline, and today its quiet prosperity as, many would agree, the prettiest village in the West, has depended upon these two mighty imponderables. The sea, though, with all its moods yet moves to a pattern, but the shifting of the sands is a mystery still.

The Glebe Terrier, the list of church properties, for Lelant in 1679 gives a terse but telling account of the invasion of the land by the sands of the sea. "In the Vicaridge house was one Hall one Buttery one Kitchen & two Chambers; wherein Mr Thomas Corey a former Incumbent lived till the Sand came in thorow the said house upon his Table & into his Bed & did otherwise So molest & incomode him, that he was forced to quitt it, notwithstanding his diligent endeavours to ye contrary." Outhouses there were a barn, a stable, and "a room for keeping implements of husbandry" with a hay loft above it. "There were belonging to the said Vicaridge severall enclosed fields of good & fertill land containing by Supposition twenty acres or upwards ....There was heretofore .... another Church .... between the sea & the blown sand: & the Present Church alsoe is extreamly damnified by the same meanes: the one halfe therof being fallen & lost: and the blown sand neare the Church as also on the Vicaridge Land as high (if not higher) than the Church itself is at the present." This testimony was signed by John Hawkins Vicar, Arth Edwards, John Hawking and "the sign of Edmund Uren", church-wardens.

A passage in the 1727 terrier baldly states, "House & glebe: none within the memory of man: all the Glebe Lands covered by an immense Quantity of Sand blown in upon them from the Sea."

At Trevethoe Gates, Lelant, 1902: Victory celebrations at the end of the Boer War
(Photograph by S. & J. Govier, courtesy RIC)

The neighbouring gentry in 1738 contributed towards repairing and clearing the church of sand and restoring it for divine service, while in 1835 on a site given by Squire Praed of Trevethoe the vicar, Rev. U. Tonkin, got a worthy vicarage at last. It is the building amid trees half way down Lelant Hill and has lately been converted into flats, the modern vicarage of less formidable proportions replacing it nearby.

Rev. Tyacke, who succeeded Mr Tonkin, and for thirty-two years until his death shortly before Christmas 1901 was Vicar of Lelant, was much admired as a power and a personality. I have heard that it was he who, with the squire, transformed sandy wasteland into the golf course which not only gives golfers one of the most magnificent views in the game, but in my 'teens enjoyed the distinction of its "Pro", Jim Barnes, winning between 1925 and '27 both the British and the American Open Championships.

My great aunts, however, thought little of Mr Tyacke's dedication to golf. They told me that when he had a funeral to conduct the parson, as he went round the course, would keep an eye on a certain bend in Church Lane. As soon as the cortège hove in sight he hurried off to the vestry to don cassock and surplice, and would meet the coffin exactly as it reached the church porch. "Timed it to a tee" you might say! On reflection it occurs to me that my beloved aunts must have entertained the very real fear that when, after a lifetime of Methodism, they came themselves to the family grave in the churchyard, Parson might not after all get to the church on time. It meant a lot to them that they should be laid to rest properly and with dignity.

Today Lelant church is a delight. For centuries after the Reformation, though, it was in a sorry state. Canon Doble presents a startling contrast.

> The church of Lelant, before the "Great Pillage" of the 16th century, with its rood-screen, its chapels and its altars, its pictures and its statues, was a dream of beauty ...: The Church was the spiritual home of the people of the parish, rich and poor, always open, a real "house of prayer" both public and private. It is sad to think of the contrast with Lelant church at the beginning of the 19th century. An old man informed the vicar about 1892 that early

in the century he had seen Lelant church full of kegs of French brandy, stored there by smugglers, who considered the church as a very safe hiding-place, because no-one would ever dream of resorting there on a weekday!

A tunnel runs from the ancient priory at Tredreath to the beach and may also have been used by smugglers. The priory is a mystery; possibly it belonged to St Michael's Mount. In 1939, at the start of the war, the tunnel was inspected as a safe shelter for the village in the event of an air raid. It proved to be chock-full of sand and was not further disturbed. There was talk of smugglers' tunnels all the way from the priory to the church too, and tunnels there were, though not primarily intended for the illicit enjoyment of the neighbourhood. Eight lodes of copper were once worked beneath Lelant, the earliest mentioned in 1580 as being in the cliff north of the church. Penaluna's Lode passes right under the church. Around 1700 the vicars of Lelant were getting fat royalties from mines on the glebe, a source of income lost when the sands blew in. You can still see adits on the beach, and it would be surprising if the "free traders" had found no use for them.

It was not just liquor, tobacco and tea that was smuggled ashore. Desperate to raise funds for the constant wars with the French, and before income tax was recognised as a well of plenty which is only now running dry, the government taxed almost every import you can think of. Searching the long list of dutiable objects you can scarcely conceive of any that escaped, at any rate on paper. Customs duties on china and earthenware, for instance, were prohibitive. Thus the tables of British Customs and Excise Duties for 1799:

China-ware, imported by the East India Company -
Home consumption duty per cent ad val.   £109.8.6
Porcelain, earthen-ware and pottery (French or
Dutch) per cent ad val.   13.4.0
Earthen-ware, not otherwise enumerated,
per cent ad val.   45.19.7
(ad val. = according to valuation)

These are duties 'way in excess of the others. They pushed up the price far beyond the purses of most people in the St Ives district; and everybody knows how a Cornish housewife "back'long" "belonged" to have a nice bit of china or two about the house, be it

The old house at Tredreath, Lelant, known as "The Abbey" and referred to by Lena Bray as the priory. This photograph by F. H. Green shows the high pavement that ran beside it in the 1920s.

never so humble. It is no wonder, therefore, that when a foreign vessel ran aground on the Lelant side of Carrack Gladden the cargo included a large quantity of china, none of it intended for the customs warehouse for which, incidentally, there was another swingeing charge. Neither is it remarkable that the ship's company were immediately hurried ashore and could not be traced, nor that the ship's papers as promptly disappeared. It was common talk that the bill of lading implicated both John Knill, Collector of Customs, and Squire Praed, for there would have been big money behind a "run" of such an expensive commodity as china.

The story ends not there, however, but with Customs Officer Roger Wearne. In his breeches, in fact! For reckoning that what was good for the master was good for the man Mr Wearne selected a few of the choicest specimens of china ware, and hid them in the seat of his small-clothes. The consequent irregularities of contour being particularly prominent as he heaved himself over the ship's side, somebody below struck him smartly behind with a stick, shattering the loot and doubtless injuring more than the officer's dignity.

But back to the church, where an even more astonishing sight was claimed to have been seen than a smuggler's cache. A sight that had nothing to do, I am assured, with the content of the kegs, even though it was Richard who saw it and not Alcey his wife. She just spread the news. But you will agree, when the tale is told, that it would have been embarrassing for a man to tell it.

Richard (of course they called him Etchart) had been to St Ives to buy fish, and buying fish in St Ives can take quite a time if you are such a stickler for a bargain as Etchart was. So it was glorious moonlight when he slogged up hill and out of town. Strange! Lelant bell was tolling. Stranger yet, it sounded muffled, not scattering the echoes as it belonged to do!

As he approached Lelant the bell was still tolling, though it tolled no louder, so leaden it rang. There were lights in the church. Curiosity mastering fear - you don't take no chances when they old free traders be about their business - Etchart peeped through a window. Nothing! Yet a glow filled the whole interior, illuminating every feature from the Norman Arch to the Pawley family, all in slate with their ruffs and fal-dals, and even the little oaken figures in the roof of the choir. Now he saw that the church was crowded with sad-faced little people wearing wreaths of the tiniest roses and carrying myrtle twigs. A procession was moving up the aisle; a funeral procession, the corpse that of a woman no bigger than the smallest doll Etchart had ever seen, and "so beautiful as if 'twere a dead seraph." Those were his very words as recorded in the page before me; they prove how poetical even an ordinary fellow like Etchart can become when wrenched by emotion. The body, he explained to Alcey through his tears, was covered with white flowers, its hair was golden threads glistening among the blossoms.

A party of little men armed with picks and shovels dug a hole close to the altar. Others lowered the body into its tiny grave. Everyone crowded round, moaning "Our queen is dead! Our queen is dead!" Suddenly one of the gravediggers tossed a shovelful of earth on to the body. At this the whole fairy host gave one wild shriek, which so alarmed Etchart that he shrieked too. At once all was plunged into darkness. Scared fairies swooped like bats in every direction and fluttered past the terrified mortal, jabbing him with needle-sharp weapons. And he fled. Lucky to make it home alive, said Alcey.

I do not know that you can see where the fairy queen was buried, but bear her in mind when you look round the church.

One day my father came home with a couple of large, parchment-covered account books. They were in manuscript, and disfigured with burn marks. He had come across a bonfire of books and papers and had succeeded in raking these two from the blaze. It had distressed him that he could save no more of this probably invaluable and certainly irreplaceable documentation. One is flowingly inscribed "Parish of Uny Lelant Vestrey Book the 4 October 1828 by John Beriman Overseer of Poor", and is endorsed on the title page by "Nathaniel Elliot Hayle Mills near Chacewater, Gwenap". The second volume, in impressive legal calligraphy, is entitled "Copy Uny Lelant Rent Charge" and is dated 7th November 1839.

I have given these two books to the Record Office, Truro.

The "Vestrey" Book covers fifty years of the history of Lelant within its scarred covers; in greater detail at the beginning when it was new, than at the end when fading pencillings, rough sums and a scribble or two occur. It is the minute book of the Parish Council, dealing with everything from nominations for church-wardens to paying John James five shillings for "picking and spalling stone in Lelant Town". One entry is entirely a church matter. The minute reads, "At a Vestry Meeting held at the Vestry Room in this Parish on Wednesday September 20th 1871 at 7 p. m. for the purpose of considering the offer of an organ for the use of the Parish Church made by Mrs. Tyacke, it was proposed by Mr. John Brush and seconded by Mr. John Bennetts that this offer be accepted and carried unanimously." Lest you might consider that the offer would better have been recorded with appreciation and gratitude than as a bare statement of acceptance, a footnote emphasises the financial nature of the transaction. "Mrs. Tyacke's offer referred to in the above Resolution is:- That she will place the organ containing 16 stops in the Parish Church of St Uny Lelant, and will remove the one now there. The organ so placed to remain her private property and to be taken from the Church at her pleasure or at that of her executors. Mrs. Tyacke undertakes that when her organ is removed it shall be replaced by one similar to the one now there containing four stops, or such an one as the parishioners may wish provided the cost does not exceed £80 to be built by Telford and Telford of Dublin or by some good organ builder. Mrs Tyacke will hand over her organ on receipt of £135." She was the vicar's wife.

The Parish Council was in every respect a local authority. It met in the vestry and had a court house at Tredreath, at a place called Hampton Court - I do not know why. The Council officers were chosen from the parishioners, the busiest of them all being the Overseers of the Poor; for much of the council's efforts and expenses were directed to caring for the needy within its borders, as the Poor Laws required. In September 1830, for example, the "weekly pay to the poor" amounted to £3.12.9 - not excessive! but it is a sum that bears no relation to the same amount today.

31 families and individuals drew a dole varying from one to five shillings a week; 2/4 on average. This was supplemented where thought necessary by relief in cash and kind. Thus in 1835 Mary Williams was drawing 1/9 a week pay, and being sick was allowed leeches and relief that cost the parish a further 5/1 . Mary Pearce also drew 1/9, and got on appeal a gown, a handkerchief and stockings to the value of 6/2. On another occasion Mary Bryant was supplied with brandy and gin; we are not told why. But the decision about James Gall speaks for itself. "James Gall, Clothing to go to Church. To have a new coat if he goes to church three Sundays following from this time."

The vestry meetings were not always drab affairs. "To Gin for Vestry Room" in 1832 - £1.3.9. The councillors stumped up 6/6, the balance going to the account. Among the coals and soap, "cloam", pots for fish, a tea kettle, and all the other consumables and replacements and replenishments for the poor house occurs the monthly entry "snuff and tobacco". Good Christian charity? Or a spur to good conduct and a whip, by its witholding, to bad? The poor house was rented at 11/4 for two years. In February 1832 the parish was supporting ten "base" children. So the list goes on!

With reform in the air Parliament directed the attention of the parishes of England to health and hygiene. Lelant parish council accordingly appointed, on 5th September 1832, a Board of Health of fifteen members, including Squire Praed and two surgeons, and directed its attention to "scouring out the Cess Pools and Catch Pits, and to removing all nuisances prejudicial to Health, & further to promoting Cleanliness in the Houses and Persons of the Poor of this Parish." For this purpose, "the sum of Thirty Pounds is placed at their Disposal to be hereafter accounted for to the Parish, and the Overseers of the Poor are hereby directed to furnish the same when required."

A national network of macadamised highways financed by turnpike tolls was spreading over the country. An Act charging local government with the responsibility of making and maintaining highways stimulated road building activities from Lands End to John o' Groats. Thus in four months from June to

Lelant Parish Church

Parish of } ...... pay to the Poor
Uny Lelant } from the 25 of April to the
22 of May 1829 by Wm Quick
Overseer.

		£	s	d
4 weeks pay to Ann Thomas at 2/0 p week		"	8	0
do Elizth Arthur at 2/0 p week		"	8	0
do Mary Stevens at 2/0 do		"	8	0
do Ann Kelway at 2/3 do		"	9	0
do Lois Richards at 2/6 do		"	10	0
do Jane Hosking at 2/0 do		"	8	0
do Elizth Morley at 2/0 do		"	8	0
do Benjn Curgenven at 2/0 do		"	8	0
do Mary Thomas at 2/0 do		"	8	0
do Mary Uren @ 1/6 do		"	6	0
do Jane Uren hains @ 2/0 do		"	8	0
do William Edwards Fam @ 2/0 do		"	8	0
do Cath Briant @ 2/0 do		"	8	0
do Wm Stevens Fam @ 2/0 do		"	8	0
do Mary Edwards @ 2/6 do		"	10	0
do Jane Richards @ 2/0 do		"	8	0
do Phillis Uren's Fam @ 4/6 do		"	12	0
do Joan Carbines @ 2/0 do		"	8	0
do Thos Curgenven @ 2/0 do		"	8	0
do John Thomas Fam @ 3/0 do		"	12	0
do Honour Trewothow @ 2/0 do		"	8	0
do Phillis Hampton @ 5/0 do	1	0	0
do Elizth Congdon @ 2/0 do		"	8	0
do Mary Williams @ 1/6 do		"	6	0
do Cath Richards @ 2/0 do		"	8	0
do Phillis Arthur @ 1/0 do		"	4	0
do Sarah Briant @ 7/6 & lodis —		"	9	0
do Richd Sampson @ 4/0 do		"	16	0
do Richd Harris Wife @ 2/0 do		"	8	0
do Richd Briant @ 2/0 do		"	8	0
		£13	12	0

An extract from the Lelant Parish Vestry Book

103

October 1848 Lelant spent no less than £113.11.9 on road improvement. This gave work to many whom the parish would otherwise have had to support. There was "spalling", stone-cutting, everywhere and stone was taken from all over the parish, but by the '60s costs were getting out of hand while rates evasion had become a problem.

In June 1875 a notice appeared in the village issued by the "Clerk of the Penzance Union, in which the said Parish of Uny Lelant is situate." It required the ratepayers of the parish to elect a School Board in accordance with the Elementary Education Act of 1870. This had already been discussed in council, not noticeably with enthusiasm. The resolution was that "this Vestry thinks it is desirable to form a School Board for the Parish of Uny Lelant but considers it unnecessary that more than one central school should be built and strongly objects to be joined to any other Parish." The school was built in Church Road, and learning came in Lelant to those financially debarred from dames' schools and private tuition. It was closed down nearly a hundred years later and is now a pair of "semi-detached" - a gracious, well proportioned granite building as most of our old Cornish "board schools" still are, though many no longer serve the needs of children.

As in the middle ages so in the 19th century the church of Uny Lelant dominated Lelant parish. Parish Council and "The Vestry" were identical, one of the two churchwardens being Chairman of the Council, with Rev. Uriah Tonkin - once a vicarage had been provided for him - and then Rev. Tyacke its guiding spirit. Indeed on occasion the vicar took the chair. But throughout the district that is now Greater St Ives chapel was as vital to the community as the church, even more vital in places. Its influence on Lelant was significant, if not to the same extent as in St Ives with its non-sectarian Borough Council, or in Carbis Bay where there had been no church.

Lelant had two chapels. The Methodist chapel at Lelant Town was built in 1859 but is no more. I never knew it. That at Tredreath in Lower Lelant, with "Wesleyan Chapel built AD 1834" carved into its granite façade and surmounted by an unusual clock tower - no longer with us, alas! - serves an active congregation to this day. It had been to Lelant that Charles Wesley, the poet of Methodism, had ridden "over the stronde" from Hayle, so initiating the Evangelist brothers' missions to what was at first a hostile and unpredictable corner of Cornwall. It was to Lelant that John Wesley once crossed perilously in a coach. Some present at the consecration of the first and now the only chapel in Lelant would have heard John Wesley preach, while brother Charles's hymns still ring the rafters there.

Lelant-Hayle Ferry, about 1900

CHAPTER IX

SANDS AND SQUIRES

The Hayle River, in its dim past a ready route due south to Mediterranean tin traders awaiting business at the Mount, had always been an obstacle to east-west travel until the causeway you bowl along from Carnsew to Griggs Quay was built in 1825. Estuary and river were once wide enough to bring sea-going ships right up to the pack-bridge at St Erth; and here is where you would cross if bound for Penzance or, before 1284 when Penzance first gets a mention, Madron. It was a long way round, though, to get to St Ives. For horsemen, light carts and the over-venturesome coach there were ways across the sands at low tide. Foot travellers preferred to take the Lelant-Phillack ferry boat, and its use continued to about twenty years ago, when Ferryman Jack Couch gave up an unremunerative job.

Those "Three Miles of Golden Sands" advertised at Hayle today were popular long before the Great Western Railway brought trippers to the St Ives beaches, which served unsanitary purposes until modern refinements moved in. My grandfather, for instance, had the first bathroom in St Ives, and people used to call round to look at it. Picnickers from St Ives would walk along the coast path to catch the Lelant ferry: people thought nothing of a long walk in those days. Once you were on the Phillack side, there was nothing but sea and sand and the green, rolling towans. Not a house in sight! Mrs Raymont tells how her aunt Mary Morton was gayest of a picnic party when they crossed to Phillack sands, but wrapped in gloom when they returned. A sudden summer storm was sending the waves tumbling over the bar, and everyone remembered that many years before, on such a crossing, both the ferryman and his son had been drowned. The drowned man's ageing successor remembered too, but he stood by his obligation to get the party back to Lelant. "Who was that," he asked when all had scrambled ashore, "who began so nemble and went away all to nawthin'?"

For walking to Foundry you were put off the ferry at "the Hard", on the tip of the spit of land which projects into the estuary between the Penpol and Hayle rivers. A memorable experience was when, towards the end of the first world war, my mother heard that Clark's shop in Foundry Square had received an allotment of dried fruit. So we walked all the way from Chyangwheal to Lelant ferry. Ferryman Pomeroy rowed us across, and we returned in triumph with half a pound of currants.

The ferry boat was moored at the foot of the church path which leads under the low railway bridge to the beach. Long ago you would have walked down Lelant Churchtown street to climb aboard, passing the cemetery which the cutting disturbed in 1877; and indeed the ferry service had operated for as long as you usually mean by "always". Above the mooring stood the ferryman's hut. A modern, summer residence replaces the curious construction of ship-board timbers which I recall, and which had replaced in its turn the tarry, up-turned barge where ferryman Tom Whatty sheltered when not at the oars. It was not an unusual feature at the time for an old, worn-out keel to exchange the sea-bed for the sunshine and the rain. Before the railway came you could, as E. W. Cooke's picture shows, have seen similar fishermen's huts on today's holiday beach at Carbis Bay. It was a use a hulk could be put to, just as you will find in old-time farmyards clapped-out jallopies serving nowadays as chicken coops. Tom Whatty's hens, though, were kept behind his hut. At twopence for the full crossing and a penny for the Hard he needed an extra source of revenue.

Up to my time, when ordinary rowing boats were preferred, praams were favoured for the crossing; they could be made by the ferryman himself. They were flat-bottomed after the Norwegian pattern, their slanting bows projecting at the landings beyond the water's edge and giving the passengers a dry step aboard or ashore.

Barepta Beach (later to be called Carbis Bay) in 1848
(Drawing by E. W. Cooke, courtesy RIC)

Mrs Dolly Roach, who lived at Glenside in Church Road, brought the ferry to life as she chatted in her trim and cosy sitting room. Tom Gall Whatty, ferryman in the 1870s, was her grandfather. He met his death when, a rip tide running, two quarrelling sea captains crossing in his boat behaved with such violence as to upset it. All three were drowned. Mrs Roach's father, by nature and inclination a scholar and a naturalist, took over the ferry at the age of sixteen. His keen observation of birds and fish attracted the praise of W. H. Hudson in his book "The Land's End", published a year after Tom had died of pneumonia in 1910. Mrs Roach told of a friendship her father struck up with a young seal. "There was a big storm, and a baby seal was stranded in the river. It became great friends with father - used to come on behind the boat just like a dog. One day a sportsman was crossing the ferry. Father said, 'Look at my baby seal!' At once the sportsman up with his gun and shot it; its brains were all over the wake. He cried, father did. He cried."

Ferryman Whatty did for the Hayle estuary what today the inshore rescue boat, the helicopter and the lifeguards do. He rescued either from the boat or after diving overboard more victims of the dangerous tides and currents than will ever be told. A prized possession of his daughter was the gold watch Hayle people presented to her father for rescuing the occupants of a boat which capsized on the bar. This was in 1909, a year before Tom Whatty's death.

One of his jobs had been to tend the two red lamps that indicated the depth of water under keel. This involved a couple of hours' extra work in the "early hours", and sometimes he handed over the task to his son and two daughters. The family lived at Rose Villa in Church Road, and walking in the dark between the two churchyards on the way to the river was a nerve-tightening experience. Each of the Whatty girls had a dinghy bearing her name. Mrs Roach recalled countless trips in the *Dorothy* to the shops at Foundry. Sometimes she would digress to pass the swimming pool, reputed to be sixty feet deep, under the railway arch where the Park-and-Ride platform now is.

Mrs Roach, who was a "V.A.D." during the '14 -'18 war and had followed her father and her grandfather in

devoted service to their native Lelant, had another tale to tell. Her aunt, Nursing Sister Ivy Burt, was a close friend of Nurse Cavell, shot by the Germans for organising an escape route for British, Belgian and French soldiers trapped behind the Kaiser's lines. Edith Cavell was matron of a hospital in Brussels, and when in 1912 and 1913 she was on furlough in England she would leave Sister Burt in charge. Mrs Roach treasured several revealing letters the martyred nurse sent her aunt in those happier days; also another cherished watch which was a personal inscribed gift from Nurse Cavell. Most historic of all these souvenirs is a telegram sent to Mrs Cavell and given to Sister Burt by the bereaved but proud parent. "Edith died yeaterday heard by wire from Brussels." Edith Cavell had been executed by a German firing squad on 11th October 1915. So did that cruel volley stir an echo in little Lelant.

As for the Lelant ferry, on Tom Whatty's death in 1910 his cousin Tom Pomeroy took over the oars throughout the war. Then came Jack Couch, a worthy successor who saw the next war through.

Prior to the causeway, horsemen and transport with no other means of reaching St Ives than by the St Erth pack-bridge would make their way to Lelant across the "stronde". There were several crossings over the mud and sand that were reasonably safe for riders and carts. Coaches, though, were liable to stick in the mud or overturn as they negotiated the rocky track. A favoured route started at the old Standard Inn, formerly known as the Passage House, in Hayle. It is still as busy a pub as ever, though its patrons no longer fortify themselves, while awaiting the ebb, to wade and struggle and "Woa there!" and "Gee up!" across mud flats and through soft sand. White poles were planted to guide through the shallows and clear of quicksands. They are marked on the old Ordnance maps.

This route must have been the Pedna Crook Passage. Pedna Crook (crok = gallows) means Gallows Point. Pirates were customarily executed in sight of the scene of their crimes, the sea; and Pedna Crook may have been Lelant's "Execution Dock". I have yet to read a recorded case, though. However, in the eighth century the Cornish had repelled a Saxon invasion in the Hayle estuary. Very likely, "pour décourager les